MUNICH

POCKET GUIDE 2025

Your Essential Guide to Must-See Sights, Local Culture, and Hidden Gems

Globetrail Guides

TABLE OF CONTENTS

SCAN THE QR CODE

- Open your phone's camera.
- Point it at the QR code.
- Wait for the notification.
- Tap the link or prompt.
- Follow the instructions.

INTRODUCTION

Munich had always been on my list of places to visit, but it wasn't until 2024 that I finally made the trip. I had spent years visiting islands, soaking in the sun and sea, but I wanted something different this time. I wanted history, culture, and the charm of a city I'd never experienced before. Munich gave me all that and more.

The moment I arrived, the city greeted me with cool air and a sense of excitement. Stepping out of the train station, I was surrounded by the buzz of people, the beauty of old buildings, and a rhythm that felt alive. It didn't take long for me to fall in love with the place.

One of the first things I did was visit Marienplatz, the heart of Munich. The New Town Hall stood tall, its stunning architecture drawing everyone's eyes. At noon, I joined the crowd to watch the famous Glockenspiel, with its figures spinning and dancing to chimes. It was like stepping into a piece of living history, and I couldn't help but smile as I watched.

But it wasn't just the sights that impressed me it was the atmosphere. Munich has a way of making you feel welcome, whether you're a tourist or a local. I spent an afternoon in a traditional beer hall, sharing a table with friendly strangers who quickly became friends. The food was delicious, with giant pretzels, sausages, and beer that was some of the best I've ever tasted. The laughter and conversation around me made the experience even better.

Another highlight of my trip was the Englischer Garten. This huge park felt like an escape from the busy city streets. The trees were full of autumn colors, and the calmness of the place was perfect for a quiet walk. I even got to see surfers riding the waves on the Eisbach River a sight I never expected in a city like Munich! It's moments like these that make Munich feel special, where you can stumble upon something unique at any time.

I also explored the grand Nymphenburg Palace, wandered through the artistic streets of Schwabing, and found hidden cafes in Haidhausen. Every corner of Munich has something to discover, from historic sites to modern shops and restaurants.

As my time in Munich came to an end, I realized how much the city had surprised me. I had come expecting to enjoy myself, but I left with memories I'll never forget. It's a city that offers so much whether you're into history, food, nature, or just want to experience something new.

If you're planning a trip to Munich, this book will be your perfect companion. Inside, you'll find everything you need to make your visit unforgettable tips on where to go, what to see, and how to experience the best of this amazing city. Trust me, Munich has something for everyone, and with this guide, you're sure to make the most of your time there.

CHAPTER 1: DISCOVERING MUNICH

When you arrive in Munich, one of the first things you'll notice is how the city effortlessly blends history and modern life. From the historic streets of the Altstadt (Old Town) to the bustling modern shops and galleries, Munich offers a little bit of everything. Picture yourself standing in **Marienplatz**, the heart of the city, where the New Town Hall's Gothic architecture towers over you, but just around the corner, trendy cafés and boutiques offer a taste of Munich's contemporary side.

Munich is famous for its relaxed but lively atmosphere. The locals, known for their Bavarian hospitality, welcome you with a smile. Don't be surprised if you find yourself sharing a table with strangers at one of Munich's many beer gardens.

Augustiner Bräustuben, for instance, is a favorite among locals, where sharing stories over a cold brew is a must.

If you're a history buff, you'll love exploring landmarks like the **Nymphenburg Palace** or the **Munich Residenz**, both reminders of the city's royal past. Art lovers will feel right at home in **Schwabing**, a neighborhood known for its bohemian flair and galleries. If modern culture is more your speed, you can check out exhibitions at the **Pinakothek der Moderne**, where contemporary art takes center stage.

No trip to Munich would be complete without a visit to the **Englischer Garten**, one of the world's largest urban parks. It's the perfect spot for relaxing after a day of sightseeing. You can even watch locals surfing on the **Eisbach River**—a unique sight in the middle of a bustling city!

Ultimately, Munich is a city that offers visitors a chance to experience both its traditional charm and modern energy, making it a destination that you'll want to explore again and again.

A Brief History and Significance of Munich

Munich's rich history dates back to 1158 when it was founded by Henry the Lion, Duke of Saxony. Initially a small settlement along the Isar River, the city grew rapidly, largely due to its strategic location on key trade routes. As the seat of the powerful Wittelsbach dynasty, Munich became a political and cultural hub of Bavaria, a role it continues to play to this day.

The city's growth was not without challenges. It faced numerous conflicts, including the Thirty Years' War and heavy bombing during World War II. Despite significant destruction, Munich was meticulously rebuilt, with many of its iconic landmarks restored to their original grandeur. Today, you can walk through the reconstructed **Marienplatz** or visit the **Frauenkirche**, whose twin towers dominate the skyline and symbolize the city's resilience.

Munich has also played a significant role in German culture and politics. It was the birthplace of the Beer Hall Putsch in 1923, a failed coup attempt by Adolf Hitler. However, Munich has shed that dark chapter of its history, emerging as a beacon of tolerance and cultural celebration.

In modern times, Munich is a key player in Germany's economy, thanks to its robust tech and automotive industries, as well as being the headquarters of major companies like BMW and Siemens. It's a city that has managed to stay at the forefront of innovation while keeping its rich heritage alive.

Why Visit Munich in 2025?

2025 is an exciting time to visit Munich, with several events and cultural highlights lined up that make the city even more appealing. One of the most anticipated events of the year is the **Munich Opera Festival**. Known for its stunning performances, the festival 2025 will celebrate its 150th anniversary, with world-class productions of Mozart's **Don Giovanni** and other operatic masterpieces. It's the perfect occasion for music lovers to immerse themselves in Munich's thriving classical scene.

Of course, no mention of Munich would be complete without **Oktoberfest**. In 2025, the world's largest folk festival will return with even more grandeur. The beer tents, traditional Bavarian costumes, and lively parades will draw millions from across the globe. But what makes 2025 special is the addition of new events celebrating the festival's long history, offering visitors a deeper dive into this beloved tradition.

In addition, Munich will host the **Mega Marsch**, a 100-kilometer challenge that takes participants through Bavaria's stunning landscapes. If you're looking for an active adventure, this event will let you experience Munich and its surrounding areas in an entirely new way.

Whether you're visiting for festivals, the arts, or just the chance to enjoy Bavarian hospitality, 2025 promises to be a memorable year in Munich, with new attractions and events adding to its already extensive list of things to see and do.

How to Use This Guide

This guide is designed to help you navigate Munich with ease, ensuring you don't miss any of the city's key attractions or experiences. Whether it's your first time visiting or you're returning for another adventure, the information is structured to provide both practical travel tips and cultural insights.

Start by exploring the **Attractions** section, which lists must-see sights like **Marienplatz**, **Nymphenburg Palace**, and the **English Garden**. For each attraction, you'll find practical details like operating hours, entry fees, and the best times to visit to avoid crowds.

Next, enter the **Local Culture** section, where you'll learn about Munich's traditional festivals, food, and lifestyle. This section will help you get acquainted with the local customs, such as how to enjoy a beer at a traditional beer garden or how to navigate the city's excellent public transportation system.

For those seeking more practical advice, the **Travel Tips** section covers everything from budgeting and safety to language tips and local etiquette. This will help you feel more confident as you explore the city, ensuring a smooth and enjoyable trip.

Finally, the guide includes several suggested **Day Trips** and **Itineraries**, perfect for those looking to explore beyond Munich. Whether you have a few days or a week, this guide will help you make the most of your stay, ensuring you leave with memories that will last a lifetime.

CHAPTER 2: TOP ATTRACTIONS IN MUNICH

Marienplatz and the Glockenspiel

W hen visiting Munich, one attraction you absolutely cannot miss is **Marienplatz** and the famous  **Glockenspiel**. Located in the heart of the city's Old Town, Marienplatz has been Munich's central square since 1158, serving as a vibrant hub for public events and celebrations. It's here, at the Neues Rathaus (New Town Hall), where you'll find the Glockenspiel, an intricate mechanical clock that performs daily.

The **Glockenspiel** is much more than just a clock—it's a piece of living history that has been captivating visitors for over a century. Installed in 1908, it reenacts two key moments from Munich's past: the wedding of Duke Wilhelm V in 1568, complete with a jousting tournament, and the Schäffler dance, which was performed by barrel makers to lift the city's spirits after a devastating plague. Watching the life-sized figures spin and twirl is truly a magical experience, and the chiming of its 43 bells adds to the atmosphere.

Best Time to Visit

The Glockenspiel performs every day at **11 a.m.** and **12 p.m.**, with an additional show at **5 p.m.** from March to October. The performance lasts about 12-15 minutes, and crowds often gather, so I recommend arriving a bit early to secure a good spot. If you want an insider tip, you can also view the show from one of the higher floors of the Hugendubel bookstore nearby, which offers an elevated perspective without the crowds.

Practical Information

Watching the Glockenspiel is free, as Marienplatz is a public square. However, if you want to enjoy a panoramic view of Munich, you can ascend the tower of the New Town Hall. The ticket for the tower is around **€5** for adults and **€3** for children. The tower is accessible via elevators, making it convenient for all visitors. The Neues Rathaus is located at **Marienplatz 8, 80331 Munich**, and it's easy to reach via public transportation. The **Marienplatz station** is served by both **U-Bahn (U3 and U6)** and **S-Bahn (S1 - S8)** lines.

What to Do Nearby

Marienplatz itself is surrounded by other fascinating attractions. You can explore the **Old Town Hall (Altes Rathaus)**, which dates back to the 15th century, or visit the **Viktualienmarkt**, a famous daily food market just a short walk from the square. If you're looking for a more historical experience, climb the **St. Peter's Church** tower for another fantastic view of the city, or stroll along **Kaufingerstraße**, Munich's premier shopping street.

Where to Eat

If you're feeling hungry, there are plenty of dining options around Marienplatz. Traditional Bavarian cuisine can be enjoyed at local beer halls or restaurants nearby, where you can try dishes like **Weisswurst** (white sausage) or a giant **Bavarian pretzel**. For a casual snack, stop by **Viktualienmarkt**, which offers a variety of local delicacies and street food.

Best Time of Year

Marienplatz is a year-round destination, but one of the best times to visit is during the winter holiday season when the famous **Christmas market** takes over the square. The festive lights, mulled wine, and holiday atmosphere create an unforgettable experience. Summer is also ideal, as the Glockenspiel performs at 5 p.m., and the weather is perfect for outdoor activities.

Marienplatz and the Glockenspiel are just the beginning of what Munich offers. This guide will provide you with all the tips and recommendations you need to make your trip to Munich truly unforgettable.

Nymphenburg Palace:

When visiting Munich, Nymphen burg Palace is a top attraction you simply cannot miss. Located in the west of the city, about 5 km from the center, this grand baroque palace  stands as one of the largest in Europe, offering a fascinating blend of history, architecture, and nature. Originally built in 1664 as a summer residence for Elector Ferdinand Maria and his wife, the palace has since expanded into an enormous complex, surrounded by lush gardens, canals, and smaller park palaces that make it a magical place to explore.

A Rich History and Stunning Architecture Nymphenburg Palace was commissioned as a gift to celebrate the birth of the heir to the throne, Max Emanuel. Its original baroque design by Agostino Barelli was later enhanced in the rococo and classical styles, giving the palace its current grandeur. As you walk through the palace, don't miss the breathtaking **Steinerner Saal (Stone Hall)**, with its stunning ceiling frescoes and intricate detailing, which has remained unchanged since 1758. This hall is where Bavaria's famous King Ludwig II, also known as the Swan King, was baptized.

What to Do at Nymphenburg Palace There's so much to see within the palace grounds that you'll need at least half a day to truly take it all in. Explore the opulent rooms inside the palace itself, then make your way to the **Marstallmuseum**, home to one of the world's finest collections of royal carriages and sleighs. For art lovers, the **Museum of Nymphenburg Porcelain** showcases exquisite works crafted over the centuries.

Take a walk in the sprawling **Nymphenburg Palace Park**, which covers over 500 acres. You can explore romantic little buildings like the **Amalienburg**, a hunting lodge with an ornate Hall of Mirrors, or the **Brandenburg**, a baroque bathhouse. The park is also home to the **Botanical Garden**, perfect for a peaceful stroll amidst rare plants and flowers. During the summer, take a gondola ride along the palace's central canal for a unique view of the gardens.

Practical Information for Your Visit Nymphenburg Palace is open year-round. From April to October, the palace is open from 9 a.m. to 6 p.m., and from October to March, it operates from 10 a.m. to 4 p.m. The palace is closed on certain holidays, including Christmas, New Year's Day, and Carnival Tuesday.

Entry to the palace costs €15 from April to mid-October, and €12 during the winter months. Tickets include access to the palace, museums, and park palaces. You can buy tickets online or at the entrance. The palace grounds are free to visit, making it a great option for budget travelers.

How to Get There The palace is easy to reach by public transport. Take **Tram 17** from Munich's central station, and in about 20 minutes, you'll arrive at the "Schloss Nymphenburg" stop, right at the palace gates. If you prefer to drive, parking is available near the palace, though fees apply.

Best Time to Visit For the best experience, visit in the spring or summer when the gardens are in full bloom and the park palaces are open. Arriving early on a weekday will help you avoid the crowds, especially if you want to enjoy a quiet gondola ride or take in the peaceful beauty of the park.

Where to Eat and Drink For a relaxing break, visit the **Schlosscafé im Palmenhaus**, located right in the palace gardens. This elegant café offers a range of dishes, including breakfast, lunch, and delicious cakes. It's closed on Mondays, but the tranquil setting makes it the perfect spot to recharge after a long day of sightseeing.

Nymphenburg Palace is not just a historical site; it's a complete experience that blends art, history, and nature. With this guide in hand, you're ready to explore every inch of this magnificent attraction and make memories that will last a lifetime.

Englischer Garten

Welcome to the Englischer Garten, Munich's sprawling urban park that feels like stepping into a green paradise. Stretching over 375  hectares, this park is not just a peaceful escape from the hustle and bustle of the city but also one of the largest city parks in the world, even bigger than New York's Central Park. Established in

1789 by Elector Karl Theodor, the park was initially designed as a military garden before being opened to the public, transforming into a beloved green space for locals and tourists alike.

What to Do and See

As you stroll through the park, the lush landscape unfolds, offering something for every visitor. If you're a history buff, don't miss the **Monopteros**, a small Greek-style temple sitting atop a hill that provides a breathtaking view of Munich's skyline. The **Chinese Tower**, another must-see landmark, is surrounded by one of Munich's most popular beer gardens, where you can enjoy a refreshing drink and Bavarian delicacies while soaking in the lively atmosphere.

For something more adventurous, head to the **Eisbach River**, where skilled surfers take on the artificial wave yes, surfing in the middle of the city! Whether you're a surfer or simply an onlooker, this unique spectacle is sure to leave you in awe.

If relaxation is more your style, the serene **Kleinhesseloher See** invites you to rent a boat and gently paddle across the lake, or simply relax by its shore with a picnic. You'll also find peaceful walking paths, open meadows for lounging, and even designated nudist areas for those who want to embrace a more liberating experience.

How to Get There

Reaching Englischer Garten is easy. The park is centrally located and accessible by public transport. The closest **U-Bahn** stations are **Giselastraße, Münchner Freiheit,** and **Universität** on lines **U3 and U6**. From there, it's just a short walk to the park's entrance.

When to Visit

Englischer Garten is a year-round destination. In spring, the park bursts to life with colorful blossoms, while summer brings outdoor activities and sunbathers. Fall offers a canvas of vibrant autumn leaves, and winter provides a tranquil, snow-covered landscape ideal for quiet walks. Each season brings its magic, making it perfect no matter when you visit.

Where to Eat and Drink

The **Chinesischer Turm** beer garden is a highlight, serving traditional Bavarian dishes like **Weißwurst** (white sausage) and **Brezn** (pretzels) alongside cold beers. If you prefer something more exotic, the **Japanese Tea House** near the southern part of the park hosts regular tea ceremonies, offering a serene and cultural experience amidst the greenery.

Travel Information

- **Location:** 80805 Munich, Germany

- **Cost:** Free entry; boat rentals and refreshments in the beer garden have varying costs (around €5–€10 for drinks, €10–€20 for meals).

- **Best Time to Visit:** Spring to autumn for outdoor activities; winter for a quieter, snowy experience.

- **Opening Hours:** Open 24/7, but specific attractions like beer gardens and boat rentals have varied hours.

Englischer Garten is not just a park it's a living, breathing part of Munich's soul, where nature, culture, and history blend seamlessly. Whether you're after relaxation, adventure, or cultural exploration, this verdant sanctuary has it all

BMW Museum and BMW Welt

If you're a car enthusiast or even just someone curious about cutting-edge technology visiting the BMW Museum and BMW Welt is an unforgettable experience.

Nestled near Olympiapark, these two iconic structures serve as a tribute to the heritage and future of BMW, offering an interactive, eye-opening adventure into the world of automobiles, engineering, and design.

BMW's Museum History:

The BMW Museum is a masterpiece of design, housed in a distinctive bowl-shaped building that resembles a race car engine. Originally opened in 1973, it was renovated in 2004 to include modern exhibitions that chronicle over 100 years of BMW's journey—from its beginnings as an aircraft engine manufacturer to its role as a leader in the automotive industry. Here, you'll discover everything from classic cars and motorcycles to prototypes of future models.

The museum is divided into themed areas that immerse you in different aspects of BMW's legacy. Whether you're captivated by the **House of Design**, showcasing how inspiration turns into stunning automobiles, or fascinated by the **House of Motor Sport**, which brings the brand's Formula 1 victories to life, there's something for everyone. Notably, one of the exhibitions explores BMW's innovations in green mobility and the future of driving—perfect for anyone intrigued by electric vehicles and sustainability.

- **Opening Hours**: Tuesday to Sunday, 10:00 AM to 6:00 PM (Closed on Mondays).

- **Cost**: €10 for adults, €7 for children under 18 and students.

- **Location**: Am Olympiapark 2, Munich.

- **How to Get There**: From Munich's central station, take the U3 line to Olympiazentrum. The museum is just a short walk from the station.

BMW Welt: A Futuristic Experience

Directly opposite the museum is **BMW Welt**, a futuristic building with striking glass-and-steel architecture that reflects BMW's commitment to innovation. It serves as a multi-purpose facility, offering a closer look  at the latest BMW models, including cars, motorcycles, and even Rolls-Royce vehicles. The building also houses interactive exhibitions and a delivery center where lucky customers receive their new BMW cars in style.

Walking through BMW Welt, you can explore the future of mobility, with exhibits focused on sustainability, electric vehicles, and cutting-edge automotive technologies. While you're there, enjoy a bite to eat at one of the on-site cafes or indulge in fine dining at **Restaurant EssZimmer**, one of Munich's top gourmet spots.

- **Opening Hours**: Monday to Saturday, 7:30 AM to midnight; Sunday and holidays, 9:00 AM to midnight.

- **Cost**: Free entry.

Tips for Your Visit

Both attractions are family-friendly, with interactive stations that will keep kids engaged for hours. If you're planning a full day, I recommend starting at BMW Welt, grabbing lunch, and then diving into the museum's rich exhibits. There's also a **BMW Lifestyle & Accessory Shop** for anyone looking to bring home a stylish souvenir.

To make the most of your visit, book tickets in advance for guided tours, especially if you want an in-depth look at BMW's history or even the production process at the nearby BMW Group Plant.

- **Website**: BMW Welt and Museum

Deutsches Museum:

If you're in Munich and even remotely curious about science and technology, the *Deutsches Museum* is an absolute must-visit. Located on Museum Island in the middle of  the Isar River, this museum is one of the largest and oldest museums in the world dedicated to science and technology. It's a treasure trove of knowledge and excitement, offering a hands-on experience for visitors of all ages. Whether you're a tech enthusiast, a history buff, or a curious traveler, the museum's vast collection will blow you away.

A Brief History

Founded in 1903 by German engineer Oskar von Miller, the museum was envisioned as a place to showcase the wonders of scientific achievements. Since opening its doors, it has grown immensely, now housing over 28,000 exhibits that span multiple fields such as physics, chemistry, aviation, and much more. Unfortunately, the museum was significantly damaged during World War II, but it was painstakingly rebuilt and modernized over the decades. Today, it continues to innovate, with new interactive exhibits and special events throughout the year.

How to Get There

The museum is located at *Museumsinsel 1, 80538 Munich*. It's easily accessible via public transportation. Take any of the S-Bahn lines to *Isartor Station*, and from there, it's just a 10-minute walk to the museum. If you prefer trams, the number 17 tram will drop you off right at the *Deutsches Museum* stop. Be aware that parking around the museum can be difficult and expensive, so public transport is your best option.

What to See and Do

The museum is so large that you could easily spend an entire day exploring its numerous exhibits. Some of the most iconic displays include:

- **The U1 Submarine**: Step inside Germany's first U-boat and get a glimpse into naval engineering.

- **The Foucault Pendulum**: Watch this mesmerizing display that visually demonstrates the Earth's rotation.

- **The First Electric Dynamo**: Invented by Werner von Siemens, this exhibit showcases the birth of electrical engineering.

- **The Planetarium**: A perfect stop for astronomy lovers, offering several demonstrations daily (for an extra fee).

Additionally, the museum is known for its interactive exhibits. From the mining industry to modern robotics, there's something here for everyone. There's even a *Kids' Kingdom*, a special area designed just for children to explore science through play.

Practical Information

- **Opening Hours**: The museum is open daily from *9:00 AM to 5:00 PM*. It's only closed on certain holidays like Christmas and New Year's Day.

- **Admission Fees**: For 2024-2025, adult tickets are priced at *€15*, while students and seniors can get in for *€10*. A family ticket (two adults and up to two children) costs *€29*. Children under 6 enter for free.

- **Website**: For up-to-date information, visit their official site.

Where to Eat and Stay Nearby

After a long day of exploring, you might want to recharge. The museum itself has a café offering light snacks and drinks, perfect for a quick break. If you're looking for more, nearby restaurants like *Viktualienmarkt* and *Marienplatz* have a range of Bavarian dishes you can indulge in, from pretzels to schnitzel.

For accommodations, consider staying close to the city center, where you can easily access the museum and other attractions. Hotels like *Hotel Torbräu* or *CORTIINA Hotel* offer comfort and convenience within walking distance.

Best Time to Visit

While the museum is open year-round, it can get crowded during peak tourist season (summer and holidays). To avoid the rush, consider visiting during weekdays or in the early morning. This will allow you to experience the exhibits at a more relaxed pace and avoid long lines at popular spots like the planetarium.

No matter when you visit, the *Deutsches Museum* will leave you inspired by the endless possibilities of science and technology.

Viktualienmarkt: Munich's Iconic Market

This is located in the heart of Munich's old town, just a short walk from Marienplatz, Viktualienmarkt is a bustling food market that has been a cornerstone of Munich's culture since 1807. Originally a humble  farmers' market, it has transformed into a beloved spot where both locals and tourists come together to explore the best of Bavarian and international cuisine. Walking through this market is a feast for the senses: the scent of fresh bread, vibrant fruits, and sizzling sausages fills the air, while the sight of colorful stalls and lively vendors adds to the energetic atmosphere.

Location and How to Get There

Viktualienmarkt is incredibly easy to reach. It's located at **Am Viktualienmarkt 3, 80331 Munich**, just a 3-minute walk from Marienplatz, the city's central square. Public transport is the easiest way to get there. You can take the U-Bahn or S-Bahn to Marienplatz station, and from there, it's a short stroll to the market. If you're driving, nearby parking garages are available but expect a bit of a challenge finding a spot during peak hours.

History and Significance

Established by King Max I Joseph in the early 19th century, the Viktualienmarkt was designed to alleviate overcrowding in the nearby Marienplatz market. Over the years, it grew from a modest setup into a sprawling 22,000-square-meter marketplace, home to around 140 stalls. It is not just a place to buy groceries; Viktualienmarkt represents Munich's culinary heritage and acts as a meeting point for the city's residents. The market is famed for its traditional Bavarian offerings and its lively beer garden, where visitors can enjoy local brews under the shade of towering chestnut trees. The maypole, adorned with figures representing Munich's trades, adds a festive touch and nods to Bavarian culture.

What to Do at Viktualienmarkt

Whether you're a foodie or just someone who enjoys exploring local culture, there's plenty to do here. Browse the endless variety of fresh fruits, vegetables, cheeses, meats, and seafood. Many vendors also sell exotic ingredients, so it's a great spot for culinary adventurers. The beer garden is a must-visit; grab a **Weißwurst** (white sausage) and a Bavarian pretzel, pair them with a local beer, and soak up the market's unique atmosphere. If you're visiting in the morning, don't miss out on the

Weißwurstfrühstück, a traditional Bavarian breakfast featuring white sausage and mustard.

When to Visit and Costs

The market is open Monday to Saturday, from **8:00 AM to 8:00 PM**, though some stalls close earlier on Saturdays. There is no entrance fee, and the cost of food and drinks varies depending on what you purchase. Expect to pay around €5–€10 for a snack or small meal at one of the stalls. To avoid crowds, it's best to visit early in the morning or later in the afternoon, especially during weekdays. If you're looking for an authentic local experience, try visiting during one of the market's seasonal festivals.

Surrounding Attractions

After exploring the market, take a short walk to nearby landmarks like the **Munich Residenz** or the **English Garden**, both within easy reach. Marienplatz, with its iconic Glockenspiel, is another nearby highlight, making the Viktualienmarkt the perfect starting point for a day of sightseeing.

Final Tips

For an enhanced experience, consider joining a guided food tour of Viktualienmarkt, which will introduce you to the market's history, its most famous vendors, and the best dishes to try. The market's vibrant atmosphere, cultural significance, and culinary offerings make it an unmissable stop on your trip to Munich

CHAPTER 3: EXPLORING MUNICH'S NEIGHBORHOODS

Altstadt (Old Town)

When you visit Munich's Altstadt (Old Town), you're stepping into the heart of the city's rich history. This neighborhood is where Munich was founded, and it's packed with iconic landmarks that make it a must-see for any traveler. Start your exploration in **Marienplatz**, the central square that's home to the famous **Neues Rathaus (New Town Hall)**. Every day, visitors gather here to watch the **Glockenspiel** a clock that performs a charming, animated show featuring life-size figures reenacting historical events.

From Marienplatz, take a short stroll to the **Frauenkirche**, the Cathedral of Our Lady, with its distinctive twin towers. This Gothic masterpiece was mostly rebuilt after WWII, but its iconic towers survived, offering panoramic views of the city if you're up for the climb. Nearby is **Peterskirche (St. Peter's Church)**, Munich's oldest parish church. Climb the 306 steps up its tower for another incredible view, this time with the Frauenkirche in the frame a great photo opportunity.

For a unique cultural experience, visit the **Viktualienmarkt**, a bustling food market that's been around since the 1800s. This isn't just a place to grab a snack; it's a cultural hotspot where locals and tourists mingle while sampling Bavarian specialties like pretzels, sausages, and cheeses. There's also a large beer garden here, perfect for a midday break.

If you're a fan of architecture and history, don't miss **Asamkirche**, a small but ornate Baroque church built by the Asam brothers in the 18th century. It's known for its intricate frescoes and decorations, making it one of the most unusual and beautiful churches in Munich. Also nearby is the **Residenz**, the former royal palace of the Bavarian monarchs. Give yourself a few hours to explore the massive complex, including the stunning **Antiquarium** and **Cuvilliés Theatre**.

Altstadt also offers excellent shopping along **Kaufingerstrasse** and **Neuhauser Strasse**, two pedestrian streets lined with international brands, local boutiques, and cafes. Whether you're a history buff, architecture enthusiast, or casual traveler,

Altstadt is packed with experiences that will keep you fascinated throughout your visit.

Schwabing: Bohemian and Artsy

Schwabing is Munich's bohemian district, known for its artistic flair and vibrant atmosphere. Historically home to artists, writers, and intellectuals, it has retained its  creative spirit while embracing modernity. Your visit here should start at the expansive **English Garden**, one of the world's largest urban parks. Locals and tourists alike flock here for a peaceful walk, and if you're visiting in the summer, you might even catch surfers riding the artificial waves on the park's river.

Schwabing's main artery is **Leopoldstraße**, a lively boulevard lined with cafes, restaurants, art galleries, and shops. Whether you're looking for a chic boutique or a quirky art store, you'll find plenty of options here. For art lovers, don't miss the **Pinakothek Museums** in nearby Maxvorstadt, where you can explore world-class collections of European art.

At night, Schwabing comes alive with its eclectic mix of nightlife. From intimate jazz clubs to vibrant cabaret theaters, there's something for every taste. **Alter Simpl**, a historic pub once frequented by literary figures, is a great place to soak in the district's bohemian roots.

For a taste of the local art scene, check out one of Schwabing's many galleries or pop-up exhibitions, often featuring works by contemporary Munich artists. Even if you're not an art aficionado, Schwabing's creative energy is infectious, making it one of the city's most exciting areas to explore.

Maxvorstadt: Culture and Academia

Maxvorstadt is Munich's cultural and academic hub, home to many of the city's top museums and universities. Start your day by visiting the **Pinakothek Museums**—three world- renowned art museums that showcase European masterpieces, modern art, and contemporary works. The **Alte Pinakothek** focuses on Old Masters like Rembrandt and Rubens, while the **Neue Pinakothek** offers an impressive collection of 19th-century art, including works by Van Gogh and Monet. If modern art is more your style, head to the **Pinakothek der Moderne**.

Maxvorstadt is also where you'll find **Ludwig Maximilian University** and **Technical University of Munich**, two of

Germany's top educational institutions. This gives the area a youthful, intellectual vibe, with plenty of students and academics populating its cafes and bars. If you're interested in history, don't miss the **NS-Dokumentationszentrum**, a museum and educational center dedicated to exploring Munich's role in the rise of National Socialism.

Maxvorstadt's streets are also home to an array of independent bookstores, art galleries, and cultural institutions, making it a haven for anyone with a passion for arts and ideas. When you need a break, the area is full of cozy cafes where you can sit back and soak in the creative energy.

Haidhausen: Bars and Cafés

Haidhausen is one of Munich's trendiest neighborhoods, known for its lively bar and café scene. Located just east of the Isar River, Haidhausen has a laid-back vibe that draws both locals and visitors looking to relax and enjoy the best of Munich's nightlife.

Rosenheimer Platz is the heart of Haidhausen, with streets radiating out filled with cozy cafes, trendy restaurants, and atmospheric bars. For a truly local experience, visit one of the **Biergärten**

(beer gardens) in the area, where you can enjoy a cold brew under the chestnut trees, often accompanied by live music. Popular spots like **Hofbräukeller** offer a great selection of Bavarian beers and hearty food.

If you're in the mood for cocktails, head to **Kellerbar**, a hidden gem located in the cellar of an old building, known for its creative drinks and intimate atmosphere. For something more casual, **Café Puck** is a beloved spot to grab coffee or a light lunch before exploring the neighborhood's many boutique shops and galleries.

At night, Haidhausen comes alive with live music venues and laid-back bars that cater to a variety of tastes. Whether you're looking for a quiet evening in a jazz bar or a lively night out, Haidhausen has it all.

Glockenbachviertel: LGBTQ+ Friendly Area

Glockenbachviertel is Munich's most vibrant and inclusive neighborhood, known for its LGBTQ+-friendly atmosphere and diverse nightlife. This area, just south of the city center, has long been a hub for Munich's LGBTQ+ community, offering a welcoming environment for everyone.

The heart of Glockenbachviertel is **Gärtnerplatz**, a beautiful square surrounded by cafes, bars, and restaurants. It's the perfect spot to people-watch while enjoying a coffee or a drink. In the evening, the square transforms into a lively meeting point for locals and visitors alike.

Glockenbachviertel's nightlife is legendary, with a wide range of clubs, bars, and parties catering to all tastes. **Prosecco Bar**, one of the neighborhood's iconic LGBTQ+ bars, is a great place to start your night. For a more energetic atmosphere, head to **NY.Club**, a popular LGBTQ+ nightclub known for its dance floor and vibrant crowd.

The neighborhood also hosts several LGBTQ+ events throughout the year, including Munich's **Pride Week** and various cultural festivals, making it a dynamic and welcoming place to explore. Whether you're here for the nightlife, the culture, or just to soak in the inclusive vibe, Glockenbachviertel offers a unique and unforgettable experience.

CHAPTER 4: MUNICH'S CULTURAL HIGHLIGHTS

Bavarian Traditions and Customs

When you visit Munich, you're stepping into the heart of Bavaria, a region steeped in centuries-old traditions that remain vibrant and alive today. The first thing that strikes visitors is the prevalence of traditional attire, especially during festivals. You'll often see locals, young and old, wearing **Lederhosen** (leather pants for men) and **Dirndls** (the elegant dress for women), even for casual occasions like Sunday brunch or a walk in the park. These outfits are not mere costumes but a symbol of Bavarian pride, representing a deep connection to their cultural heritage.

Music is another integral part of Bavarian life. From the lively **oompah bands** that fill beer halls with their brass-heavy sound to the more traditional **Zither** (a stringed instrument) perfomances, music is often accompanied by dance. If you're in town during festival season, don't miss the traditional **Schuhplattler**, a folk dance where men slap their shoes and thighs in rhythm an energetic display of Bavarian spirit.

Local customs also dictate how social interactions unfold. For example, Bavarians are known for their **Gemütlichkeit**, a concept that doesn't translate perfectly into English but refers to a state of warmth, friendliness, and good cheer. This spirit comes alive in the city's beer halls and gardens, where locals gather to share a **Maß** (liter of beer) and talk for hours.

One tradition you might not expect is the **Kocherlball**, a dance held at dawn every July at the Chinese Tower in the **Englischer Garten**. Historically, it was a gathering for Munich's cooks, servants, and housemaids, but today, it draws thousands of participants many dressed in traditional attire who come to dance in the early morning light.

Oktoberfest and Other Festivals

Oktoberfest is Munich's most famous festival and a global icon of Bavarian culture. Held annually from late September to the first weekend in October, this massive  celebration draws millions of visitors from around the world. But Oktoberfest is more than just beer; it's a celebration of **Bavarian heritage**. From the grand opening ceremony where the mayor taps the first keg with the cry of **"O'Zapft is!"** (It's tapped!) to the vibrant **costume parades**, Oktoberfest is a sensory overload of sights, sounds, and tastes.

To experience Oktoberfest like a local, avoid weekends when the festival grounds are packed. Instead, visit midweek and arrive early to secure a table in one of the famous beer tents like **Schottenhamel** or **Hacker-Pschorr**. Be sure to try the **Oktoberfestbier**, a special brew made for the festival that is stronger than typical German beers, along with traditional foods like **Schweinshaxe** (pork knuckle) and giant Bavarian pretzels.

Aside from Oktoberfest, Munich hosts numerous other festivals throughout the year. In spring, there's the **Starkbierfest**, a festival dedicated to strong beers, held at the **Paulaner am Nockherberg** brewery. The summer brings the **Tollwood Festival**, a celebration of culture and sustainability, offering art, live music, and eco-friendly stalls. In December, don't miss the famous **Christkindlmarkt** (Christmas market) at **Marienplatz**, where the smell of mulled wine and roasted nuts fills the air.

Munich's Opera and Theater Scene

Munich boasts one of the most prestigious opera houses in the world, the **Bayerische Staatsoper** (Bavarian State Opera). Established in the 17th century, this  institution continues to host world-class performances of both classical and contemporary operas. The annual **Munich Opera Festival**, held every summer, is a highlight of the season, drawing opera lovers from all over the globe to witness exceptional productions in the opulent setting of the **Nationaltheater**. If you're a fan of Wagner, Munich is the place to be, as the city played a significant role in the composer's career, and his works frequently feature on the program.

For those who prefer theater, the **Münchner Kammerspiele** is one of the most important German-language theaters in Europe, known for its avant-garde productions and top-tier talent. The **Residenztheater** is another gem, offering a mix of classic and modern plays in a stunning venue that dates back to the 18th century.

Art Galleries and Museums

Munich is an art lover's paradise, home to some of the finest galleries and museums in Europe. Start your journey at the **Pinakothek der Moderne**, which houses an  impressive collection of 20th and 21st-century art, including works by Picasso and Warhol. Nearby, the **Alte Pinakothek** features European masterpieces from the Middle Ages to the 18th century, with works by Dürer, Rembrandt, and Rubens. Don't miss the **Lenbachhaus**, famous for its collection of works by the **Blaue Reiter** group, an expressionist movement founded by Wassily Kandinsky.

If you're more interested in history and science, the **Deutsches Museum** is the largest museum of technology and science in the world, offering interactive exhibits on everything from space travel to renewable energy. For car enthusiasts, the **BMW Museum** is a must-see, showcasing the evolution of one of the world's most famous automotive brands.

Munich's Beer Halls and Breweries

No trip to Munich is complete without a visit to one of its legendary beer halls. The **Hofbräuhaus am Platzl** is perhaps the most famous, with a history dating back to the 16th century. Here, you can enjoy a  **Maß** of beer while listening to traditional Bavarian music and soaking in the lively atmosphere. If you want something more low-key, head to **Augustiner-Keller**, where locals gather under chestnut trees in one of the city's oldest beer gardens.

For a more immersive experience, visit one of Munich's breweries. The **Paulaner Brewery** offers tours that take you through the  beer-making process, from the grain to the glass. You can also learn about the **Reinheitsgebot**, the German beer purity law, which has governed Bavarian brewing since 1516.

CHAPTER 5: MUNICH'S FOOD AND DRINK SCENE

Traditional Bavarian Cuisine: What to Try

When you come to Munich, indulging in Bavarian cuisine is an essential part of your experience. This region is known for hearty, flavorful dishes that carry centuries of tradition. Whether you're wandering through a lively beer hall or sitting down at a cozy local restaurant, you'll find a variety of iconic foods worth trying.

Weisswurst is a must for any first-time visitor. These white sausages are made from veal and pork back bacon and are traditionally eaten before noon. Locals love to pair them with freshly baked pretzels, a dollop of sweet mustard, and a cold glass of Weissbier (wheat beer). The cultural significance lies in the sausages' freshness – they were historically made in the morning and eaten before they spoiled. Try Weisswurst at *Hofbräuhaus* or *Weisses Bräuhaus*, where the sausages are made in-house, offering an authentic taste.

Speaking of pretzels, Bavaria's **Brezn** is a snack you'll encounter everywhere. These large, doughy delights have a perfect balance of softness on the inside with a crunchy, salty crust. For the best green, head to the *Viktualienmarkt*, where local bakeries deliver freshly baked batches each morning.

If you're feeling adventurous, **Schweinshaxe** is another dish to seek out. This roasted pork knuckle, crispy on the outside and tender on the inside, is often served with dumplings and gravy. It's a feast for meat lovers, and you'll find it at iconic beer halls like *Augustiner-Keller* or *Löwenbräukeller*. The crackling skin and rich, savory flavors make it a memorable experience.

For something lighter yet just as satisfying, try **Obatzda**. This creamy, flavorful cheese spread is made from soft cheese, butter, paprika, and beer, often served with  pretzels. It's a favorite in beer gardens and is best enjoyed at places like *Chinesischer Turm* **or** *Hirschgarten*, where you can relax in the sun while savoring this delicious appetizer.

No Bavarian meal is complete without dessert, and **Apfelstrudel** is the perfect way to end. This delicate pastry is filled with spiced apples and raisins, often served warm with vanilla sauce or ice cream. To experience a truly exceptional Apfelstrudel, visit *Café Frischhut* or *Rischart*, where they serve some of the finest in the city.

For first-time tasters, keep in mind that Bavarian portions are generous. Start small, share dishes with friends, and be open to trying new flavors you'll quickly fall in love with the bold, comforting tastes of Bavaria. And if you're ever unsure about what to try, simply ask the locals Bavarians are always happy to share their food culture.

Best Beer Gardens in Munich

Munich is synonymous with beer gardens, and if you want to experience the city like a local, visiting one is non-negotiable. These open-air spaces are where friends and families gather to enjoy cold beer, hearty food, and the relaxed Bavarian atmosphere.

One of the most iconic beer gardens is the **Augustiner-Keller**. Situated near the city center, it's been serving locals since 1812. The beer here is brewed by Augustiner, Munich's oldest brewery, and the traditional wooden barrels used for storage add a special touch. There's a sense of history in every sip, and the lively, communal atmosphere makes it easy to strike up a conversation with the people sitting next to you. Go early in the evening to grab a spot under the chestnut trees, and enjoy a liter of their full-bodied lager with some classic Bavarian snacks.

If you're looking for something a little more tranquil, the **Hirschgarten** is a fantastic choice. Located  in a massive park, this beer garden can accommodate over 8,000 people, but its sprawling size means you can always find a quiet spot. It's the perfect place to escape the hustle of the city and enjoy a relaxed afternoon with a beer in hand. The park itself is beautiful, often filled with deer grazing nearby, which adds to the serene atmosphere. Try their house-brewed beer and bring your picnic – a tradition in many Munich beer gardens.

For a beer garden with a unique flair, visit the **Chinesischer Turm** in the English Garden. With its  distinctive pagoda tower and lively setting, it's a favorite among both locals and tourists. On weekends, you can listen to live brass bands playing traditional Bavarian music as you enjoy your beer. It's the perfect spot for soaking in the city's cultural vibes while surrounded by the greenery of one of Europe's largest urban parks.

For those seeking a lesser-known gem, the **Menterschwaige** beer garden is a bit off the beaten path but well worth the visit. Nestled along the banks of the Isar River, this family-friendly garden offers a picturesque setting. It's  popular with locals who prefer a quieter, more intimate vibe. Enjoy a refreshing Radler (beer mixed with lemonade) while sitting beneath the towering trees.

Customs at beer gardens are straightforward but important. When ordering beer, remember it's usually served in a liter-sized *Maß* glass, though smaller sizes are available. If you're in the self-service area, find a spot at one of the communal tables, grab your drink and food, and enjoy the relaxed social atmosphere. Munich's beer gardens are open during the warmer months, from spring to early autumn, with evenings being the prime time to visit. Be sure to check the weather – beer gardens close during heavy rain.

Munich's Top Restaurants and Cafes

Munich's culinary scene is as lively as its history, offering a blend of traditional Bavarian fare and international influences. Whether you're after a hearty meal, a fine dining experience, or just a cozy café to unwind, Munich has it all.

For an authentic Bavarian dining experience, head to **Zum Dürnbräu**. Tucked away in the city's Altstadt, this restaurant has been serving Bavarian classics for over 500 years. Their pork roast, dumplings, and sauerkraut are the ultimate comfort foods, made with  recipes passed down through generations. The wood-paneled dining rooms and warm atmosphere make it feel like a step back in time, perfect for enjoying a hearty meal.

If you're seeking modern Bavarian cuisine, **Schwarzreiter Tagesbar & Restaurant** offers a more contemp orary twist on traditional dishes. Located in the prestigious Hotel Vier Jahreszeiten Kempinski, this Michelin-starred restaurant is known for its  creative takes on local ingredients, blending old-world flavors with innovative culinary techniques. Their multi-course tasting menus are a journey through Bavarian gastronomy, ideal for foodies looking to explore Munich's high-end dining scene.

For something more casual, **Café Frischhut** is a local favorite. Known affectionately as *Schmalznudeln*, this bakery café serves some of the best doughnuts and pastries in the city. It's the perfect spot to stop for a coffee and a sweet treat while exploring Viktualienmarkt, Munich's famous food  market. The café has been a staple in the city for decades, offering simple, yet delicious Bavarian pastries in a relaxed setting.

Coffee lovers should not miss **Man Versus Machine**, one of the best specialty coffee shops in Munich. Located in Glockenbachviertel, this minimalist café is known for its expertly brewed coffee, sourced from independent roasters around the world. Whether you're  after a flat white or a pour-over, their attention to detail will satisfy any coffee aficionado.

For a dining experience with a view, try **Theresa Grill**. This restaurant combines top-quality meats with a sleek, modern atmosphere. Located in the heart of Munich, it's perfect for steak lovers, offering a wide selection of grilled dishes, including dry-aged beef. Their outdoor terrace is particularly lovely during the summer months, offering a peaceful setting amid the city.

Munich's food scene is rich and diverse, offering something for every taste and budget. Whether you're in the mood for traditional Bavarian fare or exploring the city's international influences, there's no shortage of great places to eat and drink.

The Oktoberfest Experience: A Guide

Oktoberfest is more than just a beer festival; it's a cultural phenomenon that has been drawing millions of visitors to Munich since 1810. If you're visiting Munich in 2025, experiencing Oktoberfest firsthand is an absolute must. Spanning from mid-September to the first weekend of October, the festival is a grand celebration of Bavarian culture, complete with traditional beer, hearty food, and lively parades.

The festival takes place at **Theresienwiese**, an enormous open space in Munich that transforms into a massive fairground, with towering beer tents, carnival rides, and food stalls as far as the eye can see. Each year, around six million people attend Oktoberfest, so it's wise to plan your visit carefully. If you want to experience the best of the festival, arriving early is key. The beer tents fill up quickly, especially on weekends. Most tents open by 10 a.m., and the earlier you arrive, the better chance you have of grabbing a prime seat.

At the heart of Oktoberfest are the **beer tents** 14 large tents and 20 smaller ones, each operated by a different brewery or organization. The largest tent, **Hofbräu Festzelt**, can hold over 10,000 people and is one of the liveliest places to enjoy beer and traditional Bavarian music. If you're looking for a more relaxed experience, the **Augustiner-Festhalle** tent is a favorite among locals, serving beer from Munich's oldest brewery in an atmosphere that feels a bit more authentic and less touristy.

As for the beer, Oktoberfest beer is a special brew made by Munich's six major breweries. It's stronger than regular beer, with an alcohol content of around 6%, so pace yourself! A liter of beer, known as a *Maß*, is the standard serving size. Be prepared to pay around €12-13 per Maß in 2025, depending on the tent. If you want a break from the beer, you can also find *Radler* (beer mixed with lemonade) or non-alcoholic options like water or soda.

To fully embrace the spirit of Oktoberfest, consider wearing traditional Bavarian attire. For men, that means **Lederhosen**, and for women, it's the **Dirndl**. You'll see plenty of locals and tourists alike donning these festive outfits, and it adds an extra layer of fun to the experience. You can buy these outfits at stores throughout Munich, or even rent them for the day if you prefer.

One of the highlights of Oktoberfest is the **parade** that kicks off the festival. Known as the **"Entry of the Oktoberfest Landlords and Breweries,"** it features horse-drawn beer wagons, brass bands, and thousands of participants dressed in traditional Bavarian clothing. This parade happens on the first Saturday of the festival, and it's worth seeing if you're in town.

When it comes to food, Oktoberfest is a feast for the senses. You'll find classics like **Schweinshaxe** (roast pork knuckle), **Hendl** (roast chicken), and **Bratwurst** (grilled sausages) served in the tents. Outside the tents, stalls offer everything from giant pretzels and roasted almonds to sweets like **Kaiserschmarrn** (shredded pancakes with raisins). Be sure to try a **Lebkuchenherz**, the colorful heart-shaped gingerbread cookies, often given as a token of affection.

For first-timers, reserving a table can be a good idea, especially if you're visiting on a busy day. Some tents accept reservations months in advance, but you can often find seats if you arrive early or are willing to wait a bit. However, it's also possible to simply walk into most tents and join others at communal tables – it's all part of the Oktoberfest camaraderie.

Finally, while Oktoberfest is famously known for beer and merrymaking, it's also family-friendly, with several attractions geared towards children, such as carnival rides, games, and special family days where beer prices are reduced, and the atmosphere is more relaxed.

Oktoberfest in 2025 promises to be as lively and memorable as ever. Whether you're there for the beer, the food, the music, or the cultural experience, you'll leave with stories to share and a deeper appreciation for Bavarian traditions.

Local Markets and Street Food

Munich's local markets and street food scene are a vibrant part of the city's culture, offering a chance to get into Bavarian flavors while exploring its bustling streets. Whether you're hunting for fresh produce, handmade crafts, or a quick bite to eat, Munich has a variety of markets and street vendors to experience in 2025.

The most famous market, and one you simply cannot miss, is the **Viktualienmarkt**, located just a short walk from Marienplatz. This market has been the heart of Munich's food scene since the 19th century and continues to be a gathering spot for locals and tourists alike. Spread across 22,000 square meters,

Viktualienmarkt is home to over 140 stalls selling everything from fresh fruits and vegetables to gourmet cheeses, meats, and flowers. If you're a foodie, this is the place to explore, as many vendors specialize in local Bavarian products like *Leberkäs* (a type of meatloaf) or *Weißwurst*.

One of the best things to do at Viktualienmarkt is to grab something fresh to eat on the spot. The food stalls offer a variety of traditional Bavarian Street food, like **Bratwurst**, which is typically served in a crispy bun with mustard. Another favorite is the **Steckerlfisch**, a skewered and grilled fish, often mackerel or trout, cooked over an open flame. You'll smell it before you see it, as the smoky aroma wafts through the air.

For something sweet, head to the pastry stands where you can try a **Schmalznudel** or **Auszogne** traditional Bavarian doughnuts that are crispy on the outside and soft on the inside. Pair it with a coffee from one of the nearby cafes for a perfect afternoon snack.

Beyond Viktualienmarkt, you'll find smaller but equally charming markets scattered throughout the city. **Elisabethmarkt**, located in the Schwabing district, is a more local affair. It's smaller than Viktualienmarkt, but offers a cozy, neighborhood vibe. The stalls here focus on fresh, high-quality produce, as well as specialty food items like Bavarian honey, freshly baked bread, and organic cheeses. If you're staying in a local apartment or just want to experience the less touristy side of Munich, Elisabethmarkt is a great spot to visit.

During the warmer months, don't miss the **Auer Dult**, a traditional Bavarian fair held three times a year at Mariahilfplatz. Part flea market, part food festival, Auer Dult offers a bit of everything. You can browse through antiques, handmade crafts, and curiosities, while enjoying traditional Bavarian Street food like **Reiberdatschi** (potato pancakes) or **Käsespätzle** (cheese noodles).

Munich also has a growing street food scene that has expanded beyond traditional Bavarian fare. You'll find food trucks and pop-up vendors offering everything from burgers and pizza to vegan options. **München Streetfood Markt** is a popular event, held periodically throughout the year, where you can sample a wide variety of international street food all in one place. This is where locals and tourists alike gather for good food and a laid-back atmosphere.

For those interested in seasonal specialties, Munich's **Christmas Markets** are not to be missed. The stalls here serve **Glühwein** (mulled wine) and **Gebrannte Mandeln** (candied almonds), which are perfect for keeping warm as you browse handmade ornaments and gifts. Each neighborhood has its market, but the one at **Marienplatz** is the most famous.

CHAPTER 6: GETTING AROUND MUNICH

Public Transportation: U-Bahn, S-Bahn, Buses, and Trams

Munich's public transportation system is efficient, and convenient, and offers multiple ways to get around the city. You'll be primarily using the U-Bahn (subway), S-Bahn (suburban trains), buses, and trams. Here's a breakdown of each and how to make the most of them.

The **U-Bahn** (underground metro) consists of eight lines that connect about 100 stations throughout the city. It's the fastest way to travel between central Munich and neighborhoods slightly further afield. Trains run frequently every 5 to 10 minutes during the day, and late into the night on weekends. You'll recognize U-Bahn stations by the blue "U" signs, and tickets can be purchased at kiosks in every station. If you're staying within the city center, Zone M will cover most trips, and the best option for tourists is a day ticket (Tageskarte), which allows unlimited travel for 24 hours.

The **S-Bahn** complements the U-Bahn, offering access to the outskirts of Munich and even the airport (Franz Josef Strauss International). The S1 and S8 lines will get you from the airport to the city center in about 35 minutes. You can transfer seamlessly between the U-Bahn and S-Bahn, and tickets are interchangeable between both. The green "S" signs mark S-Bahn stations, and they operate from early morning until late at night.

For a more scenic and slower-paced option, hop on one of Munich's **trams**. These 13 lines traverse much of the city, particularly areas not covered by the U-Bahn, like Schwabing and Haidhausen. Tram rides are ideal if you want to get a good view of the city's architecture and public squares while you travel. Buses work in tandem with trams, covering more localized routes. Both buses and trams run from early morning until around midnight, with night buses available for after-hours travel.

Tickets for public transport can be purchased from machines at every station, or you can download the **MVV app**, which makes purchasing and validating tickets much easier. Keep in mind that you must validate your ticket by stamping it at the machines before boarding—fines for traveling without a validated ticket are steep, even for tourists. The Deutschland Ticket, which costs 49 euros per month, gives you unlimited access to public transportation across Germany, including Munich, and is perfect if you're staying longer or planning side trips beyond the city.

Munich operates on an honor system, meaning there are no barriers at stations, but ticket inspectors conduct random checks, so it's important to always have a valid ticket on hand. Whether you're planning a full day of sightseeing or just need a quick trip from one part of the city to another, public transportation in Munich is straightforward and designed with convenience in mind.

Biking in Munich

Munich is one of Germany's most bike-friendly cities, and getting around by bike is not only easy but enjoyable. The city has an extensive network of dedicated bike lanes, and flat terrain makes it a breeze to explore. Cycling is one of the most popular ways to commute in Munich, both for locals and visitors.

If you're staying in the city center, renting a bike is a fantastic way to experience Munich's landmarks at your own pace. You can rent bikes from various shops or use the city's bike-sharing system, **MVG Rad**, which operates through the **MVG More** app. After downloading the app, simply find a nearby rental bike using the map, scan it with your phone, and you're ready to go. Bike rental starts from just 5 cents per minute, making it an affordable way to travel. MVG Rad bikes can be dropped off at any designated station in the city.

For day-long trips, bike rental shops around the Hauptbahnhof and Marienplatz offer full-day rentals for around 15 to 20 euros. One of the most popular places to bike in Munich is the **English Garden**, one of the largest city parks in Europe. Here, you can leisurely cycle through tree-lined paths and even stop by the beer gardens along the way.

In terms of road safety, Munich has well-marked cycling paths, but as a tourist, it's important to remember that German cyclists are serious about road rules. Always stay within designated bike lanes, follow traffic signals, and be mindful of pedestrians. If you're riding in more central areas, be cautious around tram lines, as the tracks can be tricky for inexperienced cyclists to navigate.

Another popular cycling destination is **Olympiapark**, built for the 1972 Summer Olympics. It's ideal for a scenic ride with stunning views of Munich's skyline and plenty of green space to stop for a picnic or a break. If you're feeling adventurous, a bike ride along the Isar River is a great way to experience the natural beauty surrounding Munich, with well-maintained trails leading to the outskirts.

Overall, biking in Munich is not just a practical way to get around but also a great way to immerse yourself in the city's laid-back vibe and natural beauty. Whether you're zipping through the city center or taking a leisurely ride in the parks, cycling is an excellent transportation option for exploring Munich in 2024 and 2025.

Car Rentals and Taxis

Renting a car in Munich might seem convenient, but unless you're planning day trips outside the city, it's often not necessary. Munich's efficient public transport system and bike-friendly streets make it easy to explore without the need for a vehicle. However, if you do want to rent a car for excursions to the Bavarian Alps or nearby towns, **car-sharing** services such as **SHARE NOW** are popular options. These services allow you to rent cars by the minute, hour, or day, and you can drop them off anywhere within the city limits.

For tourists looking for more traditional car rentals, companies like Hertz, Sixt, and Europcar have multiple locations in the city, including at Munich Airport and the main train station. Rentals typically cost around 50 euros per day for compact cars, but prices can vary depending on the vehicle type and length of the rental. Be aware that driving in Munich comes with challenges: parking is limited and expensive, and the city center has many pedestrian-only zones where cars aren't allowed.

If you'd prefer not to drive, taxis are a reliable but expensive option. Taxi stands are scattered throughout the city, especially at major tourist areas and transportation hubs like Marienplatz and the Hauptbahnhof. Fares start at around 4 euros, with additional charges based on distance and time. A trip across the city center might cost you anywhere from 10 to 20 euros. For easier access to taxis, you can use apps like **Free Now**, which works similarly to Uber but with traditional taxis.

Ride-sharing services like Uber are available in Munich but are less common than in other major cities. Uber operates in the city, but it mostly uses licensed taxis, so the price difference between calling a cab directly and using Uber is minimal. If you're traveling late at night or after public transport has stopped running, taxis and Uber are your best options.

When renting a car or using car-sharing services, make sure to familiarize yourself with Munich's **environmental zones**. Certain areas of the city require cars to have a green sticker (Umweltplakette), which indicates the vehicle meets emission standards. Rental companies typically provide cars with the necessary stickers, but it's always good to double-check.

In summary, unless you're venturing outside of Munich, renting a car isn't necessary, and taxis are reliable but costly. Public transport or biking is almost always the better option for getting around the city.

Walking Around Munich's Old Town

One of the best ways to experience Munich is on foot, especially in the historic **Altstadt (Old Town)**. This compact, pedestrian-friendly area is filled with landmarks, from **Marienplatz** to the **Frauenkirche**, and walking allows you to soak in the history and charm of the city at your own pace.

Start your walking tour at **Marienplatz**, the central square, where you'll find the **New Town Hall (Neues Rathaus)** and the famous **Glockenspiel**. Every day at 11 a.m. and 12 p.m., the clock tower's figurines reenact scenes from Munich's history, making it a must-see for first-time visitors. From here, it's a short stroll to the **Viktualienmarkt**, a bustling open-air market where you can grab fresh produce, local cheeses, and snacks.

As you walk further into the Old Town, you'll come across the **Frauenkirche**, Munich's iconic twin-towered cathedral. It's hard to miss and offers panoramic views of the city if you're up for climbing the tower. Another must-visit is the **Residenz**, the former royal palace of the Bavarian monarchs, which now houses several museums and stunning courtyards.

One of the joys of walking through Munich's Old Town is the opportunity to explore its narrow streets and hidden corners. The area is rich in history, with buildings dating back to the Middle Ages, and each street has its unique character. Don't miss the chance to visit **Hofbräuhaus**, the city's most famous beer hall, located just a few minutes from Marienplatz. This legendary spot has been serving beer since the 16th century and is a great place to rest your feet and enjoy a Bavarian brew.

Walking is also the best way to experience **Maximilianstrasse**, Munich's most luxurious shopping street. Lined with designer boutiques and high-end stores, it's a striking contrast to the historic surroundings of the Old Town but showcases Munich's modern flair.

The best part about exploring the Old Town on foot is that you're never far from a café or a beer garden. Whether you're looking for a quick coffee or arelax over a traditional Bavarian meal, walking through Munich's Old Town is the ideal way to immerse yourself in the city's rich culture and history. Whether you're exploring grand landmarks or meandering through cobblestone lanes, Munich's Old Town offers a captivating blend of old-world charm and modern vibrancy, all within a walkable area.

CHAPTER 7: ACCOMMODATIONS IN MUNICH

Luxury Hotels

1. Mandarin Oriental Munich

- **Location**: Neuturmstrasse 1, 80331 Munich, Germany

- **Contact**: +49 (89) 290 980

- **Website**: Mandarin Oriental Munich

- **Price**: From €1,200 per night

What the hotel offers: The Mandarin Oriental Munich combines timeless elegance with modern luxury, making it one of the most sought-after hotels in the city. With just 73 rooms and suites, guests are treated to personalized service, ensuring an exclusive and intimate experience. Each room is meticulously designed, offering luxurious amenities such as marble bathrooms, oriental touches, and state-of-the-art technology, including integrated smart lighting systems and wireless charging stations. The hotel also boasts a rooftop pool with panoramic views of the city, an iconic feature that's perfect for relaxing or enjoying a cocktail at sunset. Dining at the on-site **Matsuhisa** restaurant, by famed chef Nobu Matsuhisa, is a culinary adventure blending Japanese and Peruvian flavors. Guests can also unwind at the spa, which offers a range of treatments, or stay active at the fitness center, equipped with the latest equipment. Its location is unbeatable, steps from Marienplatz, the Bavarian State Opera, and the historic Hofbräuhaus, making it perfect for exploring Munich's cultural attractions.

History: The hotel is housed in a 19th-century building that has been transformed into a contemporary luxury retreat. Its blend of historical architecture and modern amenities offers guests a unique Bavarian charm with Mandarin Oriental's signature service excellence.

2. Hotel Vier Jahreszeiten Kempinski Munich

- **Location**: Maximilianstrasse 17, 80539 Munich, Germany

- **Contact**: +49 (89) 2125 0

- **Website**: Hotel Vier Jahreszeiten Kempinski

- **Price**: From €650 per night

What the hotel offers: As a pillar of luxury since its opening in 1858, the Hotel Vier Jahreszeiten Kempinski exudes old-world charm with modern comforts. The hotel offers 297 rooms and suites, each furnished with luxurious materials, including plush bedding, antique-style furniture, and elegant décor that reflects the grandeur of its historic setting. The spa on the top floor offers stunning views of Munich's skyline, along with a sauna, steam bath, and a heated indoor pool. The on-site restaurant, **Schwarzreiter**, offers modern Bavarian cuisine crafted from locally sourced ingredients, while the hotel's iconic **Lobby Lounge** is the perfect place to enjoy traditional afternoon tea. Its location on Maximilianstrasse puts guests right in the middle of Munich's high-end shopping district, with easy access to the Opera House and the Residenz. **History**: Established as one of Munich's oldest luxury hotels,

Kempinski Vier Jahreszeiten has a rich history tied to Bavarian royalty and the city's cultural elite. Over the decades, it has maintained its reputation for offering world-class service while evolving to meet modern luxury standards.

3. BEYOND by Geisel

- **Location**: Marienplatz 22, 80331 Munich, Germany

- **Contact**: +49 (89) 700 746 700

- **Website**: BEYOND by Geisel

- **Price**: From €1,000 per night

What the hotel offers: BEYOND by Geisel is Munich's premier luxury boutique hotel, offering only 19 exclusive rooms and suites. Located directly on Marienplatz, guests enjoy stunning views of the New Town Hall and the vibrant heart of Munich. The hotel prides itself on delivering highly personalized service, with each guest having access to a private chef and concierge. Rooms are designed in a minimalist style, featuring floor-to-ceiling windows, natural wood accents, and custom-made furniture for a modern yet warm atmosphere. The **chef's kitchen** is a unique feature where guests can dine on-demand, with meals tailored to their tastes. BEYOND also offers an exclusive wine bar and lounge where guests can unwind with a curated selection of local and international wines. **History**: The hotel is part of the family-owned Geisel group, a name synonymous with luxury in Munich. Its prime location on Marienplatz places it at the epicenter of Munich's historic and cultural attractions.

4. The Charles Hotel, Rocco Forte

- **Location**: Sophienstrasse 28, 80333 Munich, Germany

- **Contact**: +49 (89) 544 555 0

- **Website**: The Charles Hotel

- **Price**: From €650 per night

What the hotel offers: The Charles Hotel is a modern luxury hotel built in 2007 and located next to Munich's Old Botanical Garden. With 136 spacious rooms and suites, The Charles is known for its sleek and contemporary design, featuring large windows that allow natural light to flood the rooms. Each room includes luxurious marble bathrooms, heated floors, and walk-in showers, as well as high-end amenities like Nespresso machines and complimentary minibars. The **Sophia's Restaurant & Bar** offers Mediterranean-inspired cuisine, while the hotel's full-service spa includes an indoor swimming pool, sauna, and extensive treatment options. The hotel also offers a state-of-the-art fitness center and personal training services.

History: Named after Sir Rocco Forte's father, The Charles Hotel is part of the prestigious Rocco Forte Hotels collection and is recognized for blending modern luxury with traditional service excellence.

5. DO & CO Hotel Munich

- **Location**: Filserbräugasse 1, 80333 Munich, Germany

- **Contact**: +49 (89) 294 640

- **Website**: DO & CO Hotel Munich

- **Price**: From €500 per night

What the hotel offers: Located near the vibrant Viktualienmarkt, DO & CO Hotel Munich offers a chic, urban escape with 31 contemporary rooms designed for modern travelers. The hotel's rooms are outfitted with minimalist yet elegant décor, featuring high-quality materials like leather and wood. High-tech amenities include flat-screen TVs, integrated sound systems, and free Wi-Fi. The rooftop terrace bar offers panoramic views of Munich and is perfect for evening cocktails. The hotel's restaurant specializes in international cuisine, blending local Bavarian flavors with global culinary trends. **History**: Part of the DO & CO group, known for its luxury catering services, this hotel offers a stylish and modern twist on traditional Bavarian hospitality.

These detailed descriptions provide a better sense of the luxury experience each hotel offers, highlighting the unique aspects that make it stand out to tourists looking for high-end accommodations in Munich.

Budget-Friendly Stays

1. Hotel Mio by Amano

- **Location**: Sendlinger Str. 46, 80331 Munich, Germany

- **Contact**: +49 (89) 61 42 11 0

- **Website**: Hotel MIO by AMANO

- **Price**: From €98 per night

What the hotel offers: Hotel MIO by AMANO is a trendy, design-forward hotel located in the lively Old Town. It's an excellent choice for budget travelers who don't want to sacrifice style or location. Each room is equipped with essential amenities such as air conditioning, a flatscreen TV, and free Wi-Fi. The hotel features an in-house bar inspired by the nightlife scene in Berlin, making it a vibrant place to unwind after exploring the city. Rooms range from the compact 'Cozy' to the more spacious 'Roomy' category, all designed with modern flair. Guests can also enjoy a rich breakfast buffet (available at an extra charge), making it a convenient option for a quick start before sightseeing.

History: Opened by the AMANO Group, known for its stylish urban hotels, this property perfectly combines budget and design in one of Munich's most vibrant districts.

2. Augusten Hotel München

- **Location**: Augustenstr. 2, 80333 Munich, Germany

- **Contact**: +49 (89) 516 596 700

- **Website**: Augusten Hotel

- **Price**: From €95 per night

What the hotel offers: Situated just a short walk from Munich's central train station, Augusten Hotel offers a no-frills but comfortable experience. This hotel is known for its simple, modern rooms that provide all the essentials, including free Wi-Fi, flatscreen TVs, and parquet floors. The clean, minimalist design ensures that guests have a relaxing space to return to after a day of exploring. For travelers interested in culture, the Kunstareal museum district is within walking distance, offering easy access to some of Munich's top art institutions. The hotel provides a breakfast buffet for an additional cost, and the surrounding area is filled with local restaurants and cafes. **History**: Augusten Hotel is a practical and affordable option, catering primarily to travelers who value location and convenience. Its proximity to the train station makes it a great choice for those traveling in and out of Munich.

3. a & o München Laim

- **Location**: Landsberger Str. 338, 80687 Munich, Germany

- **Contact**: +49 (89) 452 357 570

- **Website**: a&o München Laim

- **Price**: From €53 per night

What the hotel offers: a&o München Laim is a budget-friendly hostel offering a range of room options, from dormitory-style beds to private family rooms. Located next to the Laim train station, it provides quick and easy access to Munich's city center and other attractions via public transportation. The rooms are simple, with parquet floors and bright color schemes, and they come equipped with free Wi-Fi and private bathrooms. Additional amenities include a 24-hour reception, a bar, and a shared lounge where guests can relax or socialize. For a small fee, guests can enjoy a continental breakfast buffet each morning, and parking is available on-site for those traveling by car.

History: Part of the a&o Hostels brand, this property is ideal for solo travelers, families, and groups seeking clean, affordable accommodations without unnecessary frills.

4. Unsöld's Factory Hotel

- **Location**: Unsöldstraße 10, 80538 Munich, Germany

- **Contact**: +49 (89) 2371 7110

- **Website**: Unsöld's Factory Hotel

- **Price**: From €120 per night

What the hotel offers: A stylish boutique hotel located near the English Garden, Unsöld's Factory Hotel combines industrial design with modern comfort. The hotel's rooms are bright and well-equipped, offering flat-screen TVs, air conditioning, and complimentary Wi-Fi. The contemporary aesthetic of the rooms and common areas provides a sophisticated yet budget-conscious option for travelers. Guests can also enjoy a daily breakfast buffet in the hotel's airy breakfast room, and there are several nearby cafes and restaurants to explore. The English Garden, one of Munich's largest parks, is just a short walk away, making this hotel a great choice for those who enjoy nature and city life in equal measure.

History: Opened recently, Unsöld's Factory Hotel is gaining a reputation as an affordable yet chic option for travelers looking to stay near both the city's historic sites and green spaces.

5. Hotel Olympia

- **Location**: Maxhofstr. 23, 81475 Munich, Germany

- **Contact**: +49 (89) 759 6143

- **Website**: Hotel Olympia

- **Price**: From €75 per night

What the hotel offers: Hotel Olympia is located on the quieter outskirts of Munich, making it an ideal option for travelers who prefer a peaceful environment while still being within reach of the city center. This budget-friendly hotel offers simple yet comfortable accommodations, with rooms equipped with private bathrooms, free Wi-Fi, and TVs. The hotel's serene location allows guests to relax after a busy day in the city, and there are nearby parks and green spaces perfect for outdoor activities. A continental breakfast is served each morning, and the hotel provides free parking for guests with cars. Public transport links make it easy to reach Munich's main attractions.

History: A family-run establishment, Hotel Olympia is perfect for budget-conscious travelers who prefer a more laid-back setting away from the city's hustle and bustle.

Mid-range Hotels: Comfort and Value

1. Hotel Torbräu

   o **Location**: Tal 41, 80331 Munich, Germany

   o **Contact**: +49 (0)89 24 234 0

   o **Website**: Hotel Torbräu

   o **Price**: From €250 per night

What the hotel offers: As one of Munich's oldest family-run hotels, dating back over 500 years, Hotel Torbräu offers a mix of historical charm and modern comfort. Located just a five-minute walk from Marienplatz, this 4-star hotel provides an ideal base for exploring Munich's Old Town. Rooms are elegantly furnished, featuring satellite TV, free Wi-Fi, and marble bathrooms with modern fixtures. Guests can start their day with a rich buffet breakfast and enjoy local Bavarian specialties at the **Schapeau** restaurant. The hotel also provides an airport shuttle service and on-site parking, making it convenient for international travelers. With a location so central, you can easily access Munich's cultural landmarks, including the Isartor and Viktualienmarkt. **History**: Established in 1490, Hotel Torbräu has been welcoming guests for centuries. Its long history is visible in the classic architectural details, but the hotel's interiors have been updated to provide modern amenities, ensuring a comfortable stay in a historical setting.

2. **King's Hotel First Class**

   o **Location**: Dachauer Str. 13, 80335 Munich, Germany

   o **Contact**: +49 (0)89 551870

   o **Website**: King's Hotel First Class

   o **Price**: From €180 per night

What the hotel offers: King's Hotel First Class offers a perfect balance between luxury and affordability. Situated close to Munich's central station, this mid-range hotel provides spacious rooms with traditional Bavarian décor, including four-poster beds and wooden accents. The rooms come equipped with modern amenities such as air conditioning, free Wi-Fi, and flat-screen TVs. Guests can relax in the hotel's cozy **Ludwig's Bar**, enjoy the sauna facilities, or indulge in a lavish breakfast buffet. Its convenient location makes it ideal for exploring nearby attractions like the Oktoberfest grounds and the shopping district of Karlsplatz.

History: Inspired by Bavarian royal traditions, King's Hotel First Class combines traditional hospitality with modern conveniences, offering a cozy, regal atmosphere at a reasonable price.

3. **Hotel Splendid-Dollmann**

   o **Location**: Thierschstrasse 49, 80538 Munich, Germany

   o **Contact**: +49 (0)89 238 080

   o **Website**: Hotel Splendid-Dollmann

   o **Price**: From €170 per night

What the hotel offers: Nestled in the Altstadt-Lehel district near the Isar River, Hotel Splendid-Dollmann is a boutique hotel housed in a 19th-century townhouse. The property exudes old-world charm with its period furniture, intricate wallpaper, and a quaint garden terrace. Rooms are elegantly appointed with comfortable bedding, flat-screen TVs, and free Wi-Fi. The hotel's library and lounge area, featuring antique books and furniture, is perfect for relaxing after a day of sightseeing. The English Garden and Deutsches Museum are within walking distance, making it an excellent option for travelers who want a peaceful stay while remaining close to central Munich. **History**: Originally built as a private residence, the Splendid-Dollmann has maintained its classic character while providing all the comforts of a modern boutique hotel. Its intimate size and personalized service ensure a welcoming and relaxing atmosphere.

4. **AdvaStay by KING's**

   o **Location**: Dachauer Str. 12, 80335 Munich, Germany

   o **Contact**: +49 (0)89 5156 7790

   o **Website**: AdvaStay by KING's

   o **Price**: From €150 per night

What the hotel offers: Designed for travelers looking for a longer stay, AdvaStay by KING's offers modern, apartment-style accommodations close to Munich's main train station and the museum district. The spacious rooms come equipped with kitchenettes, making it ideal for travelers who prefer self-catering options. Despite the home-like setup, the hotel maintains hotel-style amenities such as daily housekeeping, free Wi-Fi, and a front desk for assistance. Guests can also enjoy nearby restaurants and attractions, including the Pinakothek museums, within walking distance.

History: A newer addition to Munich's mid-range hotel scene, AdvaStay is part of the King's Hotels group, known for its Bavarian-inspired elegance combined with practical, modern comforts.

5. **Hotel Cocoon Hauptbahnhof**

   o **Location**: Mittererstrasse 9, 80336 Munich, Germany

   o **Contact**: +49 (0)89 5999 390

   o **Website**: Hotel Cocoon Hauptbahnhof

   o **Price**: From €120 per night

What the hotel offers: For travelers seeking a trendy and eco-friendly stay, Hotel Cocoon Hauptbahnhof is the perfect choice. Located near Munich's central station, this hotel features compact yet stylish rooms with a retro design, vibrant colors, and creative furnishings. Rooms are equipped with flat-screen TVs, air conditioning, and complimentary toiletries. The hotel has a focus on sustainability, with features like eco-friendly materials and energy-saving appliances. Guests can relax at the hotel's **Cocoon Lobby Bar**, which offers a laid-back atmosphere with a selection of cocktails and snacks.

History: Opened in recent years, the Cocoon Hotel chain is known for offering urban travelers a fresh and youthful atmosphere, combining sustainable living with quirky, modern design.

Alternative Accommodations: Airbnb, Apartments, and Guesthouses

1. **Aparthotel Adagio München City**

- **Location**: Schwanthalerstraße 61, 80336 Munich, Germany

- **Contact**: +49 89 143 779 21

- **Website**: Aparthotel Adagio Munich City

- **Price Range**: From €120 to €160 per night, depending on the season and room size.

Description:

Aparthotel Adagio München City offers modern serviced apartments ideal for travelers looking for longer stays or the comfort of home. Located just a 10-minute walk from Munich Central Station, it's close to popular spots like Theresienwiese, home of Oktoberfest, and within easy reach of public transport.

The hotel offers various room types, from studios to two-bedroom apartments, each equipped with a full kitchen, free Wi-Fi, and air conditioning. You'll also have access to a 24-hour fitness center, self-service laundry, and an underground garage.

The spacious, contemporary rooms are perfect for both solo travelers and families, with options to accommodate up to four guests.

What makes it special: The location is unbeatable for city exploration, with major sites like Marienplatz just a short walk or subway ride away. Whether you want to cook your own meals or enjoy the convenience of nearby restaurants, the hotel is flexible enough to suit your needs.

History: Part of the Accor Group, Adagio is known for providing comfort and practicality, making it a favorite among business travelers and families alike. The Munich branch has been updated to meet modern standards, offering a clean, minimalist design in a central but quiet part of the city.

This accommodation is perfect for those who want the space and flexibility of an apartment but with hotel-like services.

Unique aspects: The property is highly praised for its spacious apartments and excellent service, with multilingual staff catering to international guests. City Aparthotel is perfect for those wanting a mix of independence and hotel-style conveniences, like laundry facilities and optional breakfast services.

2. **Pension Lindner**

- o **Location**: Dultstrasse 1, 80331 Munich, Germany

- o **Contact**: +4989263413

- o **Website**: Pension Lindner

- o **Price**: From €120 per night

What the property offers: This charming, family-run guesthouse is located in Munich's Old Town, offering a cozy and intimate stay. Pension Lindner provides a warm, personal touch with its simple yet comfortable rooms. Free Wi-Fi is available, and guests appreciate the home-cooked breakfast served each morning. The guesthouse is within walking distance of the Viktualienmarkt, Marienplatz, and many of Munich's historical sights.

Unique aspects: Pension Lindner is well-suited for travelers who prefer a more personal, quiet, and affordable experience. It's a hidden gem in the heart of Munich, perfect for tourists who want to feel like they're staying in a home away from home. The property's quaint, traditional Bavarian charm sets it apart from larger, impersonal hotels.

3. **Maximilian Munich Apartments & Hotel**

- o **Location:**
  Hochbrückenstraße 18,
  80331 Munich, Germany

- o **Contact**: +49 (89) 2425 730

- o **Website**: Maximilian Munich Apartments

- o **Price**: From €250 per night

What the property offers: Located near the English Garden, Maximilian Munich offers spacious, luxurious apartments designed for both short and extended stays. Each apartment comes with a fully equipped kitchen, living area, and modern amenities like free Wi-Fi and flat-screen TVs. The property also boasts a beautiful inner courtyard garden where guests can relax. There is an on-site spa and wellness center, offering services such as massages and saunas, making it an excellent choice for travelers looking to combine self-catering with a

touch of luxury.

Unique aspects: This aparthotel combines the best of both worlds hotel amenities with the independence of an apartment. It's a top pick for families or those seeking a more residential experience while still being close to Munich's cultural attractions, such as the Bavarian National Museum and the nearby riverbanks of the Isar.

4. **Airbnb in Glockenbachviertel**

   - **Location**: Glockenbachviertel, Munich

   - **Price**: From €100 per night (varies by listing)

What the area offers: Glockenbachviertel is Munich's vibrant and trendy neighborhood, home to nu merous well-reviewed Airbnb options. This area is known for its lively atmosphere, with a mix

of local cafés, restaurants, and boutique shops, making it a favorite among younger travelers and those wanting to experience Munich's hip side. Airbnb accommodations in this area range from sleek modern lofts to cozy, artistic apartments. Many properties feature high ratings and reviews for cleanliness, location, and host hospitality. **Unique aspects**: Staying in an Airbnb in Glockenbachviertel allows you to live like a local in one of Munich's most creative quarters. It's ideal for travelers looking for a more authentic experience, with easy access to both nightlife and public transport and proximity to the city center.

5. **Gästehaus Am RPTC**

- o **Location**: Thalkirchner Str. 180, 81371 Munich, Germany

- o **Contact**: +49 (89) 7244 8040

- o **Website**: Gästehaus Am RPTC

- o **Price**: From €85 per night

What the property offers: Located near the Isar River, Gästehaus Am RPTC offers a peaceful and comfortable stay in a more residential area of Munich. The guesthouse provides modern, simple rooms with amenities like free Wi-Fi, private bathrooms, and access to communal kitchens. It's ideal for travelers seeking quiet surroundings while still having easy access to public transport, with the U-Bahn only a few minutes away. **Unique aspects**: This guesthouse is perfect for visitors looking for affordable accommodation away from the hustle and bustle of the city center. It's especially appealing to travelers who appreciate nature, as it's near several parks and walking trails along the Isar. The property is a popular choice for longer stays, thanks to its comfortable, no-frills atmosphere.

Family-Friendly Options

1. **Novotel München Messe**

   o **Location**: Willy-Brandt-Platz 1, 81829 Munich, Germany

   o **Contact**: +49 (89) 994 000

   o **Website**: Novotel München Messe

   o **Price**: From €140 per night

What the hotel offers: Novotel München Messe is an excellent family-friendly hotel located next to the large Riem Arcaden shopping center, perfect for families who want convenience right at their doorstep. The hotel provides spacious family rooms, equipped with modern amenities such as free Wi-Fi, flat-screen TVs, and mini-fridges. A play area for children and a video game zone ensure the little ones stay entertained, while parents can unwind at the on-site **Novo² Restaurant**, which offers Mediterranean and international cuisine. Additionally, the hotel is located next to the **Messestadt West** U-Bahn station, making it easy to explore Munich's top attractions with minimal hassle. For added convenience, parking is available, and pets are also welcome.

Why it's family-friendly: The spacious family rooms and dedicated children's areas, including a play zone and special TV channels for kids, make it ideal for families. Its proximity to public transport and a major shopping mall ensures everything a family needs is within easy reach.

2. **Eden Hotel Wolff**

   o **Location**: Arnulfstrasse 4, 80335 M unich, Germany

   o **Contact**: +49 (89) 551 150

   o **Website**: Eden Hotel Wolff

   o **Price**: From €160 per night

What the hotel offers: A historic hotel founded in 1890, Eden Hotel Wolff combines old-world charm with modern conveniences. It offers 214 elegantly designed rooms and suites, perfect for families looking for comfort in the heart of Munich. Located across from the central train station, it is ideally positioned for families who plan to explore Munich by public transport. The hotel features family rooms, interconnected suites, and a range of amenities such as highchairs, children's television networks, and even babysitting services upon request. Guests can relax in the wellness area, which includes a sauna and fitness center, or enjoy Bavarian specialties at **Restaurant Central Café**. Parking and concierge services are available for added convenience.

Why it's family-friendly: Its central location and proximity to public transport make it easy for families to navigate the city. Additionally, the wide range of amenities for kids, including babysitting services and family-friendly dining options, ensures a hassle-free stay.

3. **Hotel Laimer Hof**

    o **Location**: Laimer Strasse 40, 80639 Munich, Germany

    o **Contact**: +49 (89) 178 0380

    o **Website**: Hotel Laimer Hof

    o **Price**: From €95 per night

What the hotel offers: Located in the tranquil Nymphenburg district, near the stunning Nymphenburg Palace, Hotel Laimer Hof is a cozy, family-run boutique hotel. With just 23 rooms, it offers a personalized experience and spacious family accommodations that include interconnected rooms for added comfort. The hotel's classic Bavarian architecture, combined with its warm hospitality, makes it a great option for families who prefer a quiet, relaxing environment. Families can rent bikes from the hotel to explore the nearby palace grounds and the beautiful parks surrounding it. A buffet breakfast is available daily, and the staff is always on hand to offer personalized travel tips for exploring Munich with children.

Why it's family-friendly: Its peaceful location, away from the hustle and bustle, makes it a great retreat for families. The proximity to the Nymphenburg Palace and parks offers plenty of open space for children to play, and the hotel's intimate atmosphere ensures personalized attention to family needs.

4. **Hilton Munich Park**

   o **Location**: Am Tucherpark 7, 80538 Munich, Germany

   o **Contact**: +49 (89) 3845 0

   o **Website**: Hilton Munich Park

   o **Price**: From €180 per night

What the hotel offers: Situated right next to the lush English Garden, one of Europe's largest urban parks, H ilton Munich Park is ideal for families who love the outdoors. The  hotel offers spacious family suites with park views, and amenities such as a kid-friendly menu, highchairs, and cots for infants. Parents can enjoy the hotel's indoor pool, sauna, and fitness center while the children explore the nearby playgrounds. **Tivoli Restaurant** offers international cuisine with kid-friendly options, and during the summer, the outdoor terrace is a fantastic spot for family meals. The English Garden, located just steps away, provides endless opportunities for walking, cycling, and picnics.

Why it's family-friendly: Its location next to the English Garden allows families to enjoy outdoor activities while staying close to the city center. The spacious rooms and family-focused amenities like cots, highchairs, and kid-friendly meals make it perfect for a comfortable stay with children.

5. **Holiday Inn Express Munich City West**

   o **Location**: Friedenheimer Brücke 15, 80639 Munich, Germany

   o **Contact**: +49 (89) 4111 910

   o **Website**: Holiday Inn Express Munich City West

   o **Price**: From €90 per night

What the hotel offers: Located in the western part of Munich, Holiday Inn Express Munich City West is a budget-friendly option with modern, comfortable family suites. Each room comes with a pull-out sofa bed, perfect for children. Guests enjoy a complimentary breakfast buffet every morning, including options for kids. The hotel is well-connected by public transport, with an S-Bahn station just outside, making it easy to reach Munich's main attractions. Families can also take advantage of the hotel's free Wi-Fi, ensuring children stay entertained. The hotel has a modern, casual atmosphere, and there is a small café and bar for snacks and drinks throughout the day.

Why it's family-friendly: The combination of spacious family rooms, free breakfast, and its convenient location near public transport make this hotel an excellent choice for budget-conscious families visiting Munich.

These hotels provide a variety of family-friendly amenities and services, from on-site dining options to child entertainment, ensuring a stress-free and enjoyable stay in Munich for families traveling in 2024-2025

CHAPTER 8: SEASONAL TRAVEL IN MUNICH

Best Time to Visit Munich

When planning a trip to Munich, timing is essential because each season brings a different flavor to the city. If you're a **festival-goer**, late September to early October is your prime window to experience the world-famous **Oktoberfest**. This period is bustling, and accommodation prices skyrocket due to high demand, so early booking is essential. Along with the beer festival, the fall foliage in city parks like the **English Garden** adds a serene beauty to your walks.

For those who prefer milder weather and fewer tourists, **late spring** (May to June) is ideal. The blooming gardens, outdoor cafes, and moderate temperatures make this a great time for **culture lovers**. You can also catch the **Frühlingsfest**, a local spring festival. **Summer** (July to August) is peak tourist season, and while crowds gather, the city's beer gardens, festivals like **Tollwood Summer Festival**, and warm weather make it perfect for **outdoor enthusiasts**. However, be prepared for occasional rain and higher prices for flights and hotels.

Winter in Munich, especially during **December**, is magical thanks to the **Christmas markets** that light up the city. If you're a **fan of snowy adventures**, this season is perfect for experiencing both festive charm and nearby skiing. January and February, while cold, are ideal for budget travelers, as it's the low season with more affordable accommodation and fewer crowds.

Ultimately, **spring and early autumn** strike the perfect balance between good weather, manageable crowds, and local events, but there's truly something for every type of traveler year-round.

Summer in Munich: Festivals and Outdoor Activities

Summers in Munich are filled with lively festivals and outdoor activities that capture the city's vibrant spirit. One of the highlights is the **Tollwood Summer Festival** held from June to July. This cultural festival in the **Olympiapark** offers a mix of live music, theater performances, and international cuisine, all with an eco-friendly ethos. It's a great place to mingle with locals and experience Munich's alternative side. Another must-attend event is the **Munich Film Festival** in late June, showcasing international films in open-air cinemas across the city.

For those who enjoy outdoor activities, summer is ideal for exploring the city's lush parks. The **English Garden** is a favorite spot for both locals and tourists, offering opportunities for picnics, bike rides, and even watching urban surfers ride the waves on the **Eisbach River**. If you prefer a more tranquil setting, head to **Westpark** for a peaceful picnic or a boat ride on the lake.

Munich's famous beer gardens also come alive in summer. A visit to the **Augustiner Keller** or the **Hirschgarten**, the largest beer garden in the city, is a quintessential Munich experience. You can enjoy a cold **Maß** of local beer under the shade of chestnut trees, often with traditional Bavarian dishes like **pretzels** and **Weißwurst**.

With warm temperatures averaging 22-26°C (72-79°F), you'll have plenty of daylight to explore the city. Just keep in mind that summer showers are common, so pack an umbrella. Whether you're into festivals, parks, or relaxing with a beer, summer in Munich offers endless ways to enjoy the outdoors.

Autumn Highlights: Oktoberfest and Beyond

Autumn in Munich is synonymous with **Oktoberfest**, the world's largest beer festival, held annually from mid-September to the first weekend in October. The event takes place at the **Theresienwiese** fairgrounds and attracts millions of visitors from all over the globe. First-timers should plan: popular tents like **Schottenhamel** and **Hofbräu Festzelt** fill up quickly, so it's a good idea to reserve a table or arrive early. Beyond the beer, Oktoberfest offers traditional Bavarian music, hearty dishes like **Schweinshaxe** (pork knuckle), and amusement rides.

However, Munich in autumn is not just about Oktoberfest. The city's parks, like the **Nymphenburg Palace Gardens**, are stunning with fall foliage, offering a quieter retreat after the festival frenzy. It's also a great time to explore Munich's **harvest** festivals and **Auer Dult**, a traditional market fair in October where you can shop for crafts and enjoy fairground rides.

Autumn is also prime time for **food lovers**, with specialties like **white asparagus** in spring giving way to heartier dishes in fall. Be sure to sample **Kaiserschmarrn**, a delicious shredded pancake served with apple sauce.

With daytime temperatures between 10-18°C (50-65°F), autumn provides cooler weather that's perfect for exploring the city's outdoor attractions and cultural landmarks, including the **Deutsches Museum** or the **BMW Welt**. For those who enjoy quieter streets, late October offers fewer crowds as the Oktoberfest visitors leave, making it an excellent time to explore Munich's museums, markets, and historical sites.

Winter Wonderland: Christmas Markets and Snowy Adventures

Winter in Munich is a magical season, especially with the city's famous **Christmas markets** lighting up the streets. The largest and most famous is the **Christkindlmarkt** at **Marienplatz**, where you'll find stalls selling everything from handmade ornaments to **Glühwein** (mulled wine) and **Lebkuchen** (gingerbread). Another charming market is the **Medieval**

Christmas Market near Odeonsplatz, which recreates the atmosphere of a 14th-century market with medieval crafts and performances.

If you're looking for something a bit different, the Tollwood Winter Festival in Theresienwiese offers a unique blend of art, music, and eco-friendly shopping, alongside international cuisine. It's an alternative market with a focus on sustainability and cultural exchange.

Winter also brings opportunities for snow sports. While Munich itself doesn't get heavy snowfall, you can easily access nearby skiing resorts like Garmisch-Partenkirchen or Zugspitze, just an hour away by train. For those staying in the city, try ice skating at the Eiszauber rink in Karlsplatz-Stachus, or head to Nymphenburg Palace for ice skating on its frozen canal, a truly picturesque experience.

Indoor attractions are also popular during the colder months. Cozy up in one of Munich's many cafes or spend the day exploring world-class museums like the Alte Pinakothek or the Deutsches Museum. The festive atmosphere, combined with snowy landscapes and warm, inviting indoor spaces, makes winter an enchanting time to visit.

With temperatures ranging from -3 to 5°C (27-41°F), it's essential to bundle up. But if you love Christmas cheer, cultural activities, and snowy adventures, winter in Munich is an unforgettable experience.

Spring in Munich: Blooming Parks and Seasonal Events

Springtime in Munich is a feast for the senses, with parks and gardens bursting into bloom and the city emerging from winter hibernation. One of the most popular spots to witness the beauty of spring is the **English Garden**, Munich's largest park. As the flowers bloom and the trees come alive, locals and tourists flock here for walks, picnics, and bike rides. The **Japanese Tea House** on an island in the park offers a peaceful retreat, while the **Chinese Tower** hosts a lively beer garden where you can enjoy a cold beer in the warming weather.

Another must-visit spot in spring is the **Nymphenburg Palace Gardens**. These Baroque-style gardens are at their most stunning when the tulips, daffodils, and cherry blossoms are in full bloom. It's the perfect location for a leisurely stroll or a peaceful afternoon admiring the royal grounds.

Spring is also festival season in Munich. One of the biggest events is **Frühlingsfest**, or Spring Festival, often called the "little sister of Oktoberfest." Held at **Theresienwiese**, this family-friendly festival offers rides, games, and traditional Bavarian food and beer. If you want to experience Munich's festive spirit without the overwhelming crowds of Oktoberfest, this is the time to visit.

Spring also marks the start of **beer garden season**, which locals celebrate with the reopening of iconic beer gardens like **Hirschgarten** and **Augustiner Keller**. With temperatures ranging from 10-18°C (50-65°F), it's the perfect time to relax outdoors, enjoying a beer under the blossoming chestnut trees.

For a more cultural experience, visit Munich during the **Starkbierzeit**, or Strong Beer Festival, in March. This lesser-known festival celebrates potent, monk-brewed beers that pack a punch. It's a more intimate affair than Oktoberfest, but just as traditional.

Whether you're picnicking in a blooming park, exploring historical sites, or enjoying a beer at a festival, spring in Munich is a celebration of renewal and tradition. The city comes alive with outdoor activities, and the mild weather makes it a perfect time to visit before the summer crowds arrive.

CHAPTER 9: PLANNING YOUR MUNICH TRIP

How to Get to Munich: Flights

For international travelers, flying to Munich is one of the easiest and fastest ways to reach the city. **Munich International Airport (Franz Josef Strauss Airport, MUC)** is one of  Europe's busiest and most well-connected airports, making it a major hub for flights from all over the world.

If you're flying from North America, you'll find direct flights from major cities like New York, Chicago, Toronto, and Los Angeles with airlines such as **Lufthansa**, **United Airlines**, and **Air Canada**. Flights from **JFK Airport** to Munich, for instance, are frequent, and a typical non-stop flight takes around 8 hours.

From the U.S. West Coast, the flight from **Los Angeles (LAX)** to Munich usually takes about 12 hours. Prices for flights to Munich can vary significantly based on the season but expect to pay anywhere from $600 to $1,200 for a round-trip economy ticket from the U.S. In general, late summer and early fall, particularly during Oktoberfest, tend to see higher prices due to increased demand.

For European travelers, Munich is a well-serviced destination with multiple low-cost airlines operating routes. **Ryanair** and **EasyJet** offer budget-friendly flights from major cities like **London**, **Paris**, and **Barcelona**, often for as little as €50 if booked in advance. These airlines primarily use smaller European airports but provide convenient options for short-haul flights to Munich.

When you arrive at Munich Airport, the **S-Bahn (S1 and S8 lines)** offers a direct train connection to Munich's city center. The ride takes about 40 minutes and costs approximately €11. Trains run every 10 minutes, ensuring easy access no matter your arrival time. Additionally, the **Lufthansa Express Bus** connects the airport to the **Hauptbahnhof (Munich Central Station)**, offering another convenient option, particularly for travelers with lots of luggage. The bus fare is around €10 each way.

Munich Airport also offers excellent facilities for travelers, including an extensive range of shops, restaurants, and even a brewery called **Airbräu**, where you can sample freshly brewed Bavarian beer before heading into the city. If you're flying long-haul and need some rest before or after your journey, airport hotels like **Hilton Munich Airport** are available for convenience.

For those needing to continue their journey to other parts of Germany or Europe, Munich Airport offers excellent onward connections. You can easily catch domestic flights to cities like Berlin, Hamburg, or Frankfurt, or take advantage of international flights to popular destinations like Vienna, Zurich, or Rome. Munich is also a central hub for travel to the Alps, with seasonal flights providing easy access to winter sports resorts across Austria and Switzerland.

How to Get to Munich: Trains

Munich is a major hub in Europe's rail network, and traveling by train offers a scenic, comfortable, and eco-friendly alternative to flying. Germany's **Deutsche Bahn (DB)** operates efficient and frequent services connecting Munich with other cities in Germany and across Europe.

For those traveling domestically, Munich is well-connected to all major German cities. High-speed **ICE (InterCity Express)** trains link Munich to **Berlin** in just under 4 hours, making it a quick and convenient option. Trains from **Frankfurt** to Munich, which is about 400 km away, take around 3 hours, and tickets start from around €50 if booked in advance. **Cologne** is another popular destination, with travel times of approximately 5 hours. Booking tickets early via the Deutsche Bahn website or app often results in cheaper fares.

For international travelers, Munich's central location in Europe makes it easily accessible by train from neighboring countries. If you're coming from **Vienna**, high-speed **Railjet** trains operated by Austrian Federal Railways (ÖBB) provide a direct connection, taking about 4 hours. From **Zurich**, Switzerland, **EuroCity (EC)** trains run several times a day, and the journey takes about 4 hours. Travelers coming from **Paris** can catch the **TGV** high-speed train, which whisks you across the French-German border in just over 5 hours. Tickets for these international routes can be booked through Deutsche Bahn, as well as local railway providers like **SNCF** for France or **ÖBB** for Austria.

For shorter journeys within Bavaria, Munich is connected to nearby towns and cities via regional trains. The **Bavaria Ticket** is a great option for day trips, allowing unlimited travel on local trains (as well as buses and trams) across Bavaria for a flat rate of €27 for a single traveler, with discounted rates for groups. This ticket is perfect if you're planning visits to nearby attractions like **Neuschwanstein Castle**, **Nuremberg**, or **Salzburg** in Austria.

Munich's **Hauptbahnhof** (main train station) is located in the heart of the city, making it a convenient arrival point. The station itself is a major transportation hub, with connections to the **U-Bahn**, **S-Bahn**, trams, and buses. It's also home to a variety of shops, restaurants, and services, ensuring a comfortable wait if you have time before your train departs. If you're arriving by train, you'll be just a short walk or a few stops on public transport from key landmarks like **Marienplatz**, the **English Garden**, and **Odeonsplatz.**

For travelers looking to explore Europe further, Munich's train station offers night trains to cities like **Rome**, **Milan**, and **Budapest**, making it a convenient base for onward travel. You can also use the **Interrail** pass to travel across multiple countries, with Munich as a starting or ending point.

Visa and Entry Requirements

If you're planning a trip to Munich, it's important to be aware of the visa and entry requirements to avoid any travel disruptions. Since Germany is a member of the **Schengen Area**, the entry rules will depend on your nationality and the purpose of your visit. Here's what you need to know:

Schengen Area Overview: The **Schengen Agreement** allows for free movement between 27 European countries, including Germany. Once you enter one Schengen country, you can travel to others within the Schengen zone without undergoing passport checks at internal borders. Munich, being in Germany, follows Schengen rules for entry and visa requirements.

For EU/EEA and Swiss Citizens

If you're a citizen of the **European Union (EU)**, **European Economic Area (EEA)**, or **Switzerland**, you do not need a visa to enter Munich. All that's required is a valid passport or a national identity card. You can stay for an unlimited period, and there are no specific restrictions on working, studying, or other activities within Munich or Germany. This ease of access makes Munich an attractive destination for visitors from neighboring European countries.

For U.S., Canadian, Australian, and Japanese Citizens

If you're from the **United States**, **Canada**, **Australia**, **Japan**, or any of the other 62 countries that have visa-free travel agreements with the Schengen zone, you do not need a visa for stays of up to **90 days** for tourism, business, or family visits. However, your passport must be valid for at least **three months** beyond your planned departure date from the Schengen area. Immigration officers may ask for proof of onward travel and sufficient funds to cover your stay, so it's wise to have these documents ready.

Visa Requirements for Non-Schengen Visitors

If you're from a country that does not have a visa-free agreement with the Schengen Area, you will need to apply for a **Schengen visa** before traveling to Munich. This visa allows stays of up to **90 days** within 180 days for tourism, family visits, business, or short-term study. Schengen visa applications can be made at the German consulate or embassy in your home country. Be prepared to provide documents such as proof of accommodation, travel insurance, financial means, and an invitation letter if you're visiting family or friends.

Post-Brexit Considerations for UK Citizens

Following Brexit, **UK citizens** are no longer EU citizens, but they still enjoy visa-free access to Germany for stays of up to 90 days within a 180-day period for tourism or business purposes. However, if you plan to stay longer or work during your visit, you'll need to apply for a visa or residency permit. Make sure your passport is valid for at least **six months** beyond your stay.

ETIAS Requirement from 2024

From **2024 onwards**, travelers from visa-exempt countries (including the U.S., Canada, and Australia) will be required to obtain an **ETIAS (European Travel Information and Authorization System)** before entering the Schengen Area. This is not a visa, but a pre-authorization process that involves a simple online application and a small fee. The ETIAS will be valid for multiple entries over three years, or until your passport expires.

Important Travel Tips

- **Documents**: Always carry your passport and any necessary visas with you during your trip, as authorities may request to see them.

- **Customs**: Be sure to check any customs regulations regarding what you can bring into Germany, especially in terms of food, alcohol, tobacco, and cash limits.

- **Health Insurance**: Non-EU visitors should ensure they have adequate travel insurance that covers medical emergencies and treatment during their stay.

Itineraries: 3-Day

3-Day Itinerary: Highlights of Munich

A 3-day trip to Munich allows you to experience the city's most famous attractions, while still leaving time to enjoy its lively culture and local cuisine.

Day 1: Explore the Old Town (Altstadt)

- Start your morning at **Marienplatz**, the heart of Munich. Catch the **Glockenspiel** at 11 a.m. and visit the **New Town Hall**.

- Walk to the **Viktualienmarkt**, Munich's famous food market, where you can sample local delicacies like pretzels, sausages, and cheese. It's the perfect spot for lunch.

- In the afternoon, visit **Frauenkirche**, Munich's iconic cathedral, and then head to **Residenz Munich**, the former royal palace, for a tour of its opulent rooms.

- End your day with dinner at a traditional Bavarian beer hall like **Hofbräuhaus**.

Day 2: Museums and Gardens

- Spend your morning at the **Deutsches Museum**, one of the world's largest museums of science and technology.

- For lunch, head to **Maximilianstrasse**, where you can enjoy upscale cafes and shopping.

- In the afternoon, relax at the **English Garden**, Munich's vast park, where you can rent a paddle boat or visit one of the beer gardens.

- In the evening, dine at the **Augustiner Keller**, one of Munich's oldest beer gardens, known for its authentic Bavarian dishes and lively atmosphere.

Day 3: Day Trip to Dachau or Neuschwanstein Castle

- If you're interested in history, take a half-day trip to the **Dachau Concentration Camp Memorial Site**, located about 30 minutes from Munich by train. This visit provides an important insight into Germany's WWII history.

- Alternatively, you can visit the fairytale-like **Neuschwanstein Castle**, about a 2-hour drive from Munich, known for its breathtaking architecture and scenic alpine backdrop.

- Return to Munich in the evening and enjoy dinner at a Michelin-star restaurant, such as **Tantris**, for a fine dining experience.

This 3-day itinerary covers Munich's top sights, blending history, culture, and Bavarian culinary delights

Itinerary: 5-day Trip to Munich

A 5-day trip to Munich gives you the perfect balance between exploring the city's rich cultural heritage and venturing outside to experience some of Bavaria's most iconic day trips.

Day 1: Munich's Old Town and History

- Start your trip in **Marienplatz**, where you can catch the **Glockenspiel** performance at 11 a.m. and 12 p.m. Climb up the tower of **St. Peter's Church** for a panoramic view of Munich.

- Visit **Viktualienmarkt** for lunch. Explore the wide variety of Bavarian delicacies like sausages, pretzels, and local cheese, while also indulging in freshly brewed beer from the nearby stalls.

- In the afternoon, explore **Munich Residenz**, the grand palace of the Bavarian monarchs. Make sure to tour the **Treasury** and **Cuvilliés Theatre**.

- Wrap up the day with dinner at the historic **Hofbräuhaus**, Munich's most famous beer hall, dating back to the 16th century.

Day 2: Art and Culture

- Spend the morning at the **Alte Pinakothek**, one of the most important art galleries in the world, with works from the Middle Ages to the 18th century. Nearby, you'll also find the **Neue Pinakothek** and **Pinakothek der Moderne**, which focus on 19th-century and contemporary art, respectively.

- Have lunch at one of the many cafés in the artsy **Schwabing** neighborhood.

- In the afternoon, visit the **BMW Museum** and **BMW Welt**, where you can explore the history of one of the world's most famous car brands. This museum is a must-see for car enthusiasts and offers interactive exhibits.

- Enjoy a relaxing evening in the **Olympic Park**, built for the 1972 Olympics. You can also opt for the **Olympic Tower** for breathtaking views of the city.

Day 3: Dachau Memorial and Nymphenburg Palace

- Take a morning train to the **Dachau Concentration Camp Memorial Site**, located about 30 minutes outside of Munich. A guided tour is highly recommended to gain deep insight into this important historical site.

- After returning to the city, spend the afternoon at **Nymphenburg Palace**. Explore the lavish palace rooms, stroll through the beautiful **Nymphenburg Gardens**, and visit the **Marstallmuseum**, which houses the royal carriages.

- Have a relaxed dinner at **Schlosswirtschaft Schwaige**, a restaurant near Nymphenburg Palace serving traditional Bavarian cuisine.

Day 4: Day Trip to Neuschwanstein Castle

- Dedicate this day to a full-day excursion to **Neuschwanstein Castle**, the fairy-tale castle nestled in the Bavarian Alps. Take a 2-hour train ride to **Füssen**, from where it's a short bus ride to the base of the castle.

- After visiting Neuschwanstein, explore the nearby **Hohenschwangau Castle** or take a walk around the stunning **Alpsee Lake**.

- Return to Munich in the evening, and dine at a cozy Bavarian tavern, such as **Augustiner Keller**.

Day 5: English Garden and Shopping

- Start your last day with a visit to **The English Garden**, one of the largest urban parks in Europe. Take a stroll or rent a bike, and don't miss the **Chinese Tower Beer Garden** for a traditional Bavarian lunch.

- In the afternoon, shop along **Maximilianstrasse**, Munich's luxury shopping street, or visit **Sendlinger Straße** for more boutique stores and souvenirs.

- End your trip with a fine dining experience at **Schwarzreiter Tagesbar & Restaurant**, known for its modern take on Bavarian cuisine.

This 5-day itinerary offers a rich blend of art, history, local culture, and breathtaking excursions, giving you a well-rounded experience of Munich and its surroundings.

Itinerary: 7-day Trip to Munich

A week in Munich allows you to dive deeper into the city's attractions, explore nearby towns, and even enjoy a leisurely day trip to Salzburg or Innsbruck. This itinerary includes a perfect mix of culture, history, nature, and relaxation.

Day 1: Old Town and Marienplatz

- Start your journey in **Marienplatz** and witness the famous **Glockenspiel**. Explore the Old Town's highlights like **St. Peter's Church**, **Frauenkirche**, and the lively **Viktualienmarkt** for a Bavarian lunch.

- Spend the afternoon at the **Munich Residenz**, the sprawling former royal palace of the Bavarian kings. Visit the **Cuvilliés Theatre** and **Antiquarium** Hall.

- Dinner at **Augustiner Bräustuben**, offering an authentic Bavarian beer hall experience.

Day 2: Museum Day

- Visit the **Deutsches Museum**, one of the largest science and technology museums in the world. Spend the morning exploring its impressive exhibits.

- Afterward, visit the nearby **Museum of Urban and Contemporary Art** (MUCA) for modern artistic inspiration.

- In the evening, dine at **Tantris**, one of Munich's top Michelin-starred restaurants, offering creative haute cuisine.

Day 3: Nymphenburg Palace and Botanical Gardens

- Spend the morning exploring the opulent rooms of **Nymphenburg Palace** and its beautiful gardens. Don't miss the **Amalienburg**, a small, ornate hunting lodge in the palace park.

- Take a peaceful afternoon stroll through the **Botanical Garden**, located adjacent to Nymphenburg Palace.

- Return to the city center for dinner at **Der Pschorr**, located on Viktualienmarkt and known for its local ingredients and traditional Bavarian dishes.

Day 4: Day Trip to Salzburg

- Take a 1.5-hour train ride to **Salzburg**, Austria, the birthplace of **Mozart** and the filming location of "The Sound of Music." Explore **Hohensalzburg Fortress**, **Mirabell Palace**, and **Getreidegasse**.

- Have lunch at the famous **Café Tomaselli**, one of Austria's oldest cafés.

- Return to Munich in the evening, and enjoy a relaxing meal at **Wirtshaus in der Au**, offering Bavarian dishes in a casual setting.

Day 5: Bavarian Alps and Neuschwanstein Castle

- Take a day trip to **Neuschwanstein Castle**, Ludwig II's stunning fairytale castle. After a tour of the castle, hike around **Alpsee Lake** and enjoy the breathtaking mountain scenery.

- Optionally, visit **Hohenschwangau Castle**, just a short distance away.

- Return to Munich for dinner at **Hofbräuhaus**, where you can experience Munich's traditional beer hall atmosphere.

Day 6: English Garden and Schwabing

- Start your day with a leisurely walk or bike ride through the **English Garden**, stopping by the **Chinese Tower Beer Garden** for a traditional Bavarian lunch.

- In the afternoon, explore the vibrant **Schwabing** district, known for its artistic vibe, unique boutiques, and cafés. Visit **Leopoldstraße** for shopping or relax in one of the outdoor cafés.

- Dinner at **Schwabinger Wahrheit**, a modern restaurant offering a fusion of international and Bavarian cuisine.

Day 7: Munich's Markets and Shopping

- Spend your last day visiting Munich's bustling **markets**. Explore **Elisabethmarkt**, a local market with a wide variety of fresh produce, flowers, and handmade goods.

- Enjoy a final shopping spree along **Maximilianstrasse** for luxury brands or head to **Kaufingerstraße** for souvenirs.

- End your trip with a special farewell dinner at **Atelier**, a Michelin-starred restaurant known for its innovative and artistic cuisine.

This 7-day itinerary allows you to experience the very best of Munich, while also providing opportunities for relaxing day trips to nearby Austrian cities or the Bavarian Alps.

Packing Tips for Munich

Packing for a trip to Munich requires careful planning, especially considering its distinct seasonal changes and the types of activities you plan to engage in. Munich experiences all four seasons, so it's important to tailor your wardrobe to the time of year you're visiting. Additionally, the city is home to famous events like **Oktoberfest**, which calls for special considerations in packing. Here's what you should know to pack effectively for your Munich trip in 2024-2025.

Spring (March to May)

In spring, Munich begins to thaw out from winter, but temperatures can still be unpredictable, ranging from **5°C to 15°C** (41°F to 59°F). It's common to experience rain during this time, so **pack layers** and be prepared for sudden shifts in weather. Here's what you'll need:

- **Light jacket or windbreaker**: Something waterproof or water-resistant is ideal for spring showers.

- **Sweaters or cardigans**: Layering is key to adjusting to the changing temperatures.

- **Comfortable shoes**: Opt for water-resistant shoes for exploring the city, especially if you plan to visit parks like the **English Garden**.

- **Umbrella**: A compact travel umbrella is essential during springtime.

- **Scarf and hat**: Munich can still be chilly in early spring, so bring a scarf and hat for cooler mornings.

Summer (June to August)

Summers in Munich are warm, with temperatures ranging from **18°C to 25°C** (64°F to 77°F). Summer is also the festival season, with outdoor events and beer gardens bustling with activity. Here's how to pack:

- **Lightweight clothing**: Pack breathable fabrics like cotton and linen. T-shirts, shorts, and dresses are great for daytime wear.

- **Comfortable walking shoes**: Munich is a walkable city, and you'll likely spend a lot of time exploring landmarks like **Marienplatz** and **Nymphenburg Palace**.

- **Sun protection**: Don't forget sunglasses, sunscreen, and a hat, especially if you'll be spending time outdoors in the parks or beer gardens.

- **Light jacket or cardigan**: Even in summer, evenings can be cool, especially if you're dining al fresco at one of Munich's beer gardens.

- **Swimwear**: If you plan to visit any of Munich's lakes or the **Isar River**, pack swimwear for a quick dip.

Autumn (September to November)

Autumn in Munich is characterized by cooler temperatures, usually ranging from **10°C to 18°C** (50°F to 64°F), and it's also the season for **Oktoberfest**. Here's what you should pack for an autumn visit:

- **Layered clothing**: Bring long-sleeved shirts, light sweaters, and a medium-weight jacket.

- **Dirndl or Lederhosen**: If you're visiting for Oktoberfest, you'll want to pack or purchase traditional Bavarian attire. These outfits are widely available for purchase or rental in Munich.

- **Waterproof footwear**: Rain is common during autumn, so consider boots or water-resistant shoes for walking.

- **Warm scarf and gloves**: It can get chilly, especially in the evenings, so pack a scarf and gloves to stay comfortable.

Winter (December to February)

Winter in Munich can be cold, with temperatures dipping to **0°C or lower** (32°F or below), particularly in January and February. Here's how to pack for the colder months:

- **Warm, insulated jacket**: A down or fleece-lined jacket is essential for staying warm.

- **Thermal layers**: Bring thermal underwear and long-sleeved shirts to wear under your clothes.

- **Winter boots**: Waterproof and insulated boots are important, especially if it snows.

- **Hat, gloves, and scarf**: Don't forget these winter essentials, as Munich's cold can be biting, particularly in the mornings and evenings.

- **Holiday market gear**: If you're visiting during December, Munich's **Christmas markets** are magical, but it can get cold standing outside. Bring extra layers and warm socks.

Special Events and Day Trips

- **Oktoberfest**: In addition to traditional attire, pack casual clothing for daytime exploring, as well as something warmer for the evenings. Comfortable shoes are a must, as you'll likely be standing or walking for long periods.

- **Day Trips**: If you're planning a day trip to the **Bavarian Alps** or **Neuschwanstein Castle**, bring suitable hiking shoes and a light backpack for snacks and water.

Useful Travel Apps and Resources for Munich

When traveling to Munich, having the right apps on your phone can make your trip smoother and more enjoyable. From going around the city to finding the best local restaurants and events, these travel apps will be indispensable for visitors in 2024-2025.

1. MVV App: Public Transport

- **Why You Need It**: Munich's public transport system is extensive, and the **MVV App** (Münchner Verkehrs- und Tarifverbund) is essential for navigating it. This app covers the **U-Bahn**, **S-Bahn**, buses, and trams, providing real-time schedules, route planning, and ticket purchasing. You can buy single tickets, day passes, or group tickets directly within the app, making it easy to get around the city without worrying about finding a ticket machine.

- **Download for** iOS | Android

2. DB Navigator: Train Travel

- **Why You Need It**: If you plan to travel beyond Munich to other parts of Germany or neighboring countries, **DB Navigator** is the best app for booking and managing train travel. Operated by **Deutsche Bahn**, this app lets you check train schedules, purchase tickets, and track live departures. It's perfect for day trips to places like **Neuschwanstein Castle** or **Salzburg**.

- **Download for** iOS | Android

3. Google Maps: Navigation and Local Discovery

- **Why You Need It**: While it's a global standard, **Google Maps** excels in Munich for both navigation and discovering local businesses. You can use it to find public transport routes, walking paths, and driving directions. Google Maps also features restaurant reviews, business hours, and user photos, making it a valuable tool for finding hidden gems like **Viktualienmarkt** stalls or a cozy beer garden in the **English Garden**.

- **Download for** iOS | Android

4. GetYourGuide: Tours and Activities

- **Why You Need It**: **GetYourGuide** offers a variety of tours and activities you can book in advance or on the go. Whether you want to join a guided walking tour of **Marienplatz**, book a day trip to **Neuschwanstein Castle**, or take a beer-tasting tour during **Oktoberfest**, this app provides easy booking and user reviews to ensure a good experience.

- **Download for** iOS | Android

5. Google Translate: Language Assistance

- **Why You Need It**: While many people in Munich speak English, it's always helpful to know a bit of German, especially when visiting more local or traditional areas. **Google Translate** offers translation for text, voice, and images. You can download the German language pack for offline use, making it a handy tool when you're out and about without internet access.

- **Download for** iOS | Android

6. Time Out Munich: Events and City Guide

- **Why You Need It**: **Time Out Munich** is perfect for staying updated on local events, exhibitions, concerts, and festivals happening during your stay. It provides recommendations for things to do in real-time, whether you're looking for an art gallery opening or the best beer garden to visit that weekend.

- **Download for** iOS | Android

7. Time Out Munich: Events and City Guide

- **Why You Need It**: **Time Out Munich** keeps you updated on the city's latest events, including concerts, art exhibitions, festivals, and other cultural activities. Whether you're looking to discover the latest trendy restaurants or explore Munich's nightlife, this app is a great tool to stay in the know during your trip. You can even find recommendations for special seasonal events, such as Oktoberfest and Christmas markets.

- **Download for** iOS | Android

8. Muenchen.de: Official City App

- **Why You Need It**: For official updates on everything happening in Munich, the **Muenchen.de** app is the go-to source. It provides information on public services, events, shopping, dining, and attractions around the city. The app also includes a detailed city map and transportation guide to help you navigate Munich's streets and neighborhoods.

- **Download for** iOS | Android

CHAPTER 10: DAY TRIPS FROM MUNICH

Neuschwanstein Castle

Neuschwanstein Castle is one of the most iconic landmarks in Germany, often referred to as the " fairytale castle" because it inspired Walt Disney's Sleeping Beauty Castle. Located near the village of Hohenschwangau, about 128 km from Munich, it's perched dramatically on a hill with stunning views of the surrounding Bavarian Alps. The castle was commissioned by King Ludwig II of Bavaria in the 19th century and is a testament to his fascination with grand medieval architecture and opera.

Getting There: The journey to Neuschwanstein from Munich is part of the adventure. There are several ways to reach the castle, with the most popular being by **train**. Take a regional train from Munich Hauptbahnhof (central station) to Füssen, which takes around two hours. Once in Füssen, hop on the bus 73 or 78, which will take you to the ticket center in Hohenschwangau in about 15 minutes. If you're looking for a flexible or more scenic trip, **driving** is also an option. The journey by car takes around

1.5 to 2 hours via the A7 motorway, offering beautiful countryside views along the way.

Unique Experiences: Upon arrival, you can choose to either walk up to the castle (about a 30-minute uphill trek) or opt for the more leisurely **horse-drawn carriage** or **shuttle bus**. The interiors of Neuschwanstein are just as captivating as its exterior, though some visitors prefer the views from outside. Inside, you'll find opulent rooms such as the Throne Hall, inspired by medieval legends and Wagnerian operas. Don't miss a hike to **Marienbrücke** (Mary's Bridge), which offers the best panoramic view of the castle and is especially stunning in early morning light.

Insider Tips: Book your entrance tickets online well in advance, especially if you're visiting during the busy summer months, as same-day tickets often sell out. The guided tour of the castle's interior lasts around 35 minutes and is available in several languages. Another tip is to wear comfortable shoes, as you'll be doing a lot of walking, especially if you plan to explore the hiking trails around the area. If you're visiting in winter, check weather conditions as the paths can become slippery due to snow and ice .

Best Time to Visit: Neuschwanstein is beautiful year-round, but if you want to avoid the crowds, it's best to visit during the shoulder seasons of spring or fall. Winter can also be magical, with snow-covered landscapes adding a fairy-tale touch, but some paths, such as those leading to Marienbrücke, may be closed due to ice.

Dachau Concentration Camp Memorial Site

Located just 16 km northwest of Munich, the **Dachau Concentration Camp Memorial Site** serves as a sobering reminder of the atrocities of World War II. Established in 1933, it was the first Nazi concentration camp and became a model for all others.  Today, the site is preserved as a memorial and educational center.

Getting There: The easiest way to reach Dachau from Munich is by **train**. Take the S-Bahn S2 line from Munich Hauptbahnhof to Dachau station, which takes around 20 minutes. From there, a bus (726) will take you directly to the memorial site. Alternatively, you can take a guided tour, which often includes transportation, ensuring a hassle-free experience.

Unique Experiences: The memorial offers a profound educational experience. Upon arrival, visitors can explore the **museum**, housed in the former maintenance building, which provides an in-depth look at the camp's history through documents, photographs, and personal artifacts. Key parts of the camp, such as the **barracks**, the **crematorium**, and the **guard towers**, are open to the public. The **memorial chapels**— Catholic, Protestant, and Jewish—provide spaces for reflection. One of the most impactful elements of the visit is the **path of prisoners**, where detainees first arrived.

Insider Tips: Allow at least half a day to explore the memorial, as it is an emotionally heavy experience. Audioguides are available, but joining a **guided tour** can offer deeper insights into the camp's history and the stories of those who were imprisoned there. Dachau is a free site, but donations are encouraged to support its upkeep.

Best Time to Visit: The memorial is open year-round, but it's best to visit during the cooler months to avoid summer crowds. Keep in mind that some parts of the site are outdoors, so dress appropriately for the weather.

Salzburg, Austria: A Day in Mozart's Birthplace

Salzburg, Austria, located just over the border from Germany, is a fantastic day trip from Munich. Known as the birthplace of Wolfgang Amadeus Mozart, this charming city offers a rich history, stunning Baroque architecture, and breathtaking views of the surrounding Alps. Salzburg is also famous for its role in the classic film *The Sound of Music*, with many visitors coming to see the locations featured in the movie.

Getting There

Traveling from Munich to Salzburg is convenient, with several options available. The **train** is the most popular and scenic way to make the journey. Trains depart from Munich Hauptbahnhof (Central Station) and take about 1.5 to 2 hours, d epending on the connection. The Deutsche Bahn (DB) trains are comfortable, and the **Bayern Ticket** is the most affordable option for groups, allowing unlimited travel for the day across regional trains and buses. Alternatively, you can drive from Munich, which takes about 1.5 to 2 hours via the A8 Autobahn. If you choose this option, remember that driving in Austria requires a motorway vignette (toll sticker), which can be purchased at rest stops.

Unique Experiences

One of the first stops in Salzburg should be **Mozart's Birthplace** (Mozarts Geburtshaus), where the composer was born in 1756. Located on Getreidegasse, this house-turned-museum offers fascinating insights into Mozart's early life, with original instruments, letters, and family portraits. Afterward, head to **Hohensalzburg Fortress**, one of Europe's largest medieval castles. Accessible by funicular or a short hike, the fortress provides sweeping views of the city and surrounding mountains. The fortress houses various exhibitions, including military history and medieval weaponry.

For lovers of classical music, a **Mozart Concert** is a must. Several venues offer evening performances, including the **Mirabell Palace** and **Hohensalzburg Fortress**, where you can enjoy the works of Salzburg's most famous son. Many concerts are paired with dinner, making for a memorable cultural experience.

Salzburg's **Old Town (Altstadt)** is another highlight, with its narrow, cobblestone streets, Baroque buildings, and picturesque squares. Don't miss the **Salzburg Cathedral**, a stunning example of Baroque architecture, and **St. Peter's Abbey**, one of the oldest monasteries in Europe. For a more relaxed experience, take a walk along the Salzach River or visit the beautiful **Mirabell Gardens**, made famous by *The Sound of Music.*

Insider Tips

- **Salzburg Card**: Consider purchasing the Salzburg Card for the day. It provides free admission to many of the city's attractions, including museums and the fortress, as well as free public transportation. This card is an excellent value if you plan to visit multiple sites.

- **Dining**: If you have time for lunch, the **Sternbräu** beer garden is a great choice for traditional Austrian fare. Alternatively, enjoy a meal with a view at the **Imlauer Sky-Bar**, which offers both indoor and outdoor seating with panoramic views of the city.

- **Best Time to Visit**: Salzburg is a year-round destination, but the best times to visit are in the spring and fall when the weather is mild, and the tourist crowds are thinner. Winter offers a magical experience with the city's Christmas markets and snow-capped surroundings.

The Bavarian Alps: Hiking and Skiing

The Bavarian Alps are an ideal destination for day trips from Munich, offering both summer hiking adventures and winter skiing. Located about an hour away by train or car, the Alps provide a dramatic  change from the urban landscape, giving you access to some of the most breathtaking mountain views in Europe. Whether you're an outdoor enthusiast or simply want to enjoy the fresh Alpine air, the Bavarian Alps have something for everyone.

Getting There

You can easily reach the Bavarian Alps from Munich by train, with several regional trains heading toward popular Alpine towns such as Garmisch-Partenkirchen or Tegernsee. For example, Garmisch-Partenkirchen, home to the famous Zugspitze (Germany's tallest peak), is about 90 minutes from Munich by train. The **Bayern Ticket** is your best option for unlimited travel across regional trains and public transport, making it an affordable choice for groups or solo travelers. If you prefer driving, the trip along the A95 motorway takes about 1.5 hours and offers scenic views along the way.

Hiking in the Bavarian Alps

If you're visiting during the warmer months, the Bavarian Alps are a hiker's paradise. One of the most popular hikes is to the summit of **Jochberg**, located between **Walchensee** and **Kochelsee**. The hike takes about two hours to ascend, and the view from the top is breathtaking, with panoramas of both lakes and the surrounding peaks. For a shorter, less strenuous hike, the **Herzogstand** is accessible by a quick cable car ride, followed by a short 30-minute walk to the summit. The views from here stretch to Munich on a clear day.

For a more immersive hiking experience, consider guided tours that combine hiking with local culture. These tours often include a visit to a traditional Bavarian Mountain hut for lunch or even a stop at a local cheese dairy for a tasting of freshly made Alpine cheeses. The trails are well-maintained, making them accessible to both seasoned hikers and beginners.

Skiing in the Bavarian Alps

During winter, the Bavarian Alps transform into a skiing haven. **Garmisch-Partenkirchen** is the most famous ski resort in the region, having hosted the 1936 Winter Olympics. Skiers of all levels can enjoy the slopes here, with options ranging from beginner-friendly areas to more advanced pistes on the

Zugspitze. For those less interested in skiing, the nearby **Partnach Gorge** is a popular winter hiking destination, where you can walk through a narrow gorge surrounded by ice-covered rock formations.

If you're looking for a more laid-back winter experience, the **Seilbahn Zugspitze** gondola will take you to the summit of Zugspitze, where you can enjoy Germany's highest beer garden, panoramic views of four countries, and even sledding or snowshoeing on the glacier.

Insider Tips

- **Best Time to Visit**: The Bavarian Alps are a year-round destination. For hiking, late spring to early fall offers the best weather, while winter (December to March) is ideal for skiing and snow activities. Weekends can be busy, so plan your visit on a weekday to avoid the crowds.

- **Packing Essentials**: Whether you're hiking or skiing, sturdy footwear is a must. For winter visits, bring layers and a waterproof jacket to stay warm and dry. A camera is essential for capturing the stunning views!

- **Dining**: After a day of hiking or skiing, stop by one of the many mountain huts for a traditional Bavarian meal. Don't miss the chance to try **Schweinshaxe** (roasted pork knuckle) or **Kaiserschmarrn** (a fluffy shredded pancake) for a true taste of Bavaria.

Lake Starnberg

Lake Starnberg (Starnberger See) is one of the most popular day trip destinations from Munich, offering a perfect escape to nature just 25 km southwest of the city. Known f or its pristine waters, scenic views of the Alps, and its connection to Bavarian royalty, it's  a spot that offers both relaxation and cultural experiences. Often referred to as "Munich's Pool," Lake Starnberg is an ideal destination for swimming, hiking, boating, or simply enjoying the beautiful lakeside ambiance.

Getting There

Reaching Lake Starnberg from Munich is incredibly easy and quick. The most common option is taking the **S-Bahn** (S6 line) from Munich Hauptbahnhof (main train station) to **Starnberg Station**, which takes about 30 minutes. From the station, you can walk to the lakefront in just a few minutes. If you prefer driving, you can reach the lake by car via the A95 or A96 motorways, with the journey taking around 40 to 50 minutes. There are also numerous parking options around the lake, but public transport is the more convenient choice during weekends when the area can get busy.

Unique Experiences

Lake Starnberg offers a variety of activities depending on what you want out of your day. One of the most enjoyable ways to explore the lake is by **taking a scenic ferry ride**. The ferry service operates between multiple docking points around the lake, including stops at Possenhofen, Tutzing, and Berg, where you can explore various lakeside towns or visit the **King Ludwig II Memorial Chapel**, marking the spot where the famous Bavarian king was found dead under mysterious circumstances.

For those interested in royal history, don't miss a visit to **Rose Island (Roseninsel)**, the only island on Lake Starnberg, which can be reached by boat from Feldafing. Once a favorite retreat for King Ludwig II and Empress Elisabeth of Austria (Sisi), the island is famous for its lush gardens and romantic ambiance. It's a great spot for a leisurely walk or even a picnic.

If you prefer to be active, **bike rentals** are available around the lake, and the well-marked paths offer a pleasant way to ride along the shoreline. Alternatively, enjoy a swim at popular spots like **Percha Beach**, or for a quieter experience, head to **Ambach**, where the waters are calmer and the beach is less crowded.

Insider Tips

- **Best Time to Visit**: Summer is the prime time for enjoying water sports and swimming, but if you want to avoid the crowds, early fall is perfect for peaceful hikes and cycling. Spring is also a beautiful time to visit, with blooming gardens and mild weather.

- **Dining**: Starnberg has several excellent **beer gardens** where you can enjoy a traditional Bavarian meal with a view. A local favorite is the **Seebad Starnberg**, which offers a relaxing lakeside atmosphere and classic Bavarian fare.

- **Swimming**: Bring a swimsuit, as there are plenty of public bathing areas, especially at **Südbad Tutzing** and **Feldafing**. These areas are easily accessible by bike or on foot and offer stunning views of the Alps in the background.

Lake Starnberg is ideal for a flexible day trip where you can mix outdoor activities with leisurely lakeside dining and historical exploration. Whether you're into swimming, cycling, or just relaxing with a view, Lake Starnberg provides the perfect retreat from the city.

Lake Ammersee

Just a bit further southwest of Lake Starnberg lies **Lake Ammersee**, a quieter option for a day trip. It's known for its charming lakeside villages, serene atmosphere, and beautiful landscapes, making it a great alternative to the more frequented Starnberger See.

Getting There

Like Lake Starnberg, Lake Ammersee is easily accessible from Munich. You can take the **S8 S-Bahn** from Munich Hauptbahnhof to **Herrsching**, the main town on the eastern shore of the lake, which takes about 50 minutes. If you're driving, the journey takes around an hour via the A96 motorway.

Unique Experiences

Ammersee offers a variety of water-based activities, including **boating, paddleboarding, and windsurfing**. The town of Herrsching is the perfect base to rent equipment and enjoy a day on the water. You can also take a **scenic boat ride** across the lake, with stops at several picturesque villages along the shore, including **Diessen**, known for its beautiful Baroque church and pottery markets.

For a cultural twist, don't miss the **Andechs Monastery**, perched atop a hill just a short distance from the lake. The monastery is famous for its brewery, where monks still brew traditional Bavarian beers. After hiking up to the monastery, enjoy a hearty Bavarian meal paired with freshly brewed beer at the **Andechs Beer Garden**, which boasts stunning views over the countryside.

Insider Tips

- **Best Time to Visit**: Ammersee is perfect for summer swimming and boating, but spring and fall are also ideal for peaceful hikes and visits to Andechs.

- **Dining**: Herrsching is home to several excellent lakeside restaurants, but for a true Bavarian experience, head to the **Kloster Andechs** beer garden.

- **Cycling and Hiking**: There are scenic cycling routes around the lake, but if you're looking for a more relaxed activity, take a walk along the **Ammersee Promenade** in Herrsching, which offers beautiful views of the lake and the nearby Alps.

Regensburg: Medieval Charm

Regensburg, located on the banks of the Danube River, is a true gem of medieval architecture and history. A UNESCO World Heritage Site since 2006, this city is known for its beautifully preserved medieval Old  Town, winding cobblestone streets, a nd impressive landmarks. A day trip from Munich to Regensburg offers a glimpse into a city that blends ancient Roman history, medieval trading significance, and Bavarian culture, making it one of the most captivating destinations near Munich.

Getting There

Reaching Regensburg from Munich is easy and convenient. You can take a **train** from Munich Hauptbahnhof (central station), which takes about 1.5 hours. Trains are frequent, making it an ideal option for a stress-free journey. The **Bayern Ticket** is a great choice for affordable travel, covering regional trains and public transport in the city. If you prefer to drive, Regensburg is about 120 kilometers northeast of Munich, a straightforward 1.5-hour drive along the A93 motorway. Once in Regensburg, you'll find parking at the Parkhaus am Dachauplatz, which is near the Old Town.

Unique Experiences

Start your day by exploring **Regensburg Cathedral (St. Peter's Dom)**, a Gothic masterpiece dating back to the 13th century. Known for its striking twin spires, the cathedral's stained-glass windows and intricate interior make it a must-see. If you're lucky, you might catch the famous **Regensburger Domspatzen Boys Choir** performing during Sunday Mass. The cathedral is also home to the world's largest hanging organ.

From there, make your way to the **Old Stone Bridge (Steinerne Brücke)**. This 12th-century bridge is one of the oldest surviving stone bridges in Europe, providing incredible views of the Danube River and the city's medieval skyline. Walk across the bridge to get a fantastic perspective of the Old Town.

Next, explore **Porta Praetoria**, an ancient Roman gate built in 179 A.D. This is one of the few remaining Roman gates north of the Alps, a testament to Regensburg's long history as a key Roman military site. Continue to the **Goliath House**, a striking 13th-century building adorned with a large mural of David and Goliath, offering a glimpse into the city's artistic heritage.

For lunch, don't miss the **Wurstkuchl**, the world's oldest continuously operating sausage kitchen, where you can savor traditional Bavarian sausages and sauerkraut along the banks of the Danube. Dining at one of the picnic tables outside offers a unique, rustic experience.

If time permits, visit **St. Emmeram's Basilica**, a stunning Baroque church within the **Thurn and Taxis Palace** complex. The palace grounds also host seasonal events, including a romantic Christmas market and the Palace Festival in summer.

Insider Tips

- **Best Time to Visit**: Regensburg is beautiful year-round, but the best times are spring and fall when the weather is mild and the city is less crowded. If you visit in winter, the Christmas markets are a magical experience.

- **Local Festivals**: Plan your visit around the **Regensburg Dult**, a traditional Bavarian fair held in May and August, or the **Bürgerfest**, a local festival celebrating the city's heritage with live music, street food, and performances.

- **Getting Around**: Regensburg is best explored on foot, especially the Old Town, where the narrow streets and hidden alleys offer a glimpse into medieval life. Biking is also popular, with bike rentals available throughout the city

CHAPTER 11: PRACTICAL INFORMATION

Essential German Phrases for Travelers

When visiting Munich, knowing a few key German phrases can go a long way. While many locals speak English, showing that you've made an effort to speak their language is always appreciated. Here are some essential phrases you'll find useful during your trip:

1. **Hallo** (hah-loh) – Hello

2. **Tschüss** (chooss) – Goodbye

3. **Bitte** (bit-teh) – Please / You're welcome

4. **Danke** (dahn-keh) – Thank you

5. **Sprechen Sie Englisch?** (shpre-chen zee eng-lish) – Do you speak English?

6. **Ich hätte gern...** (eekh her-te gern) – I would like... (useful for ordering food or drinks)

7. **Wo ist die Toilette?** (voh ist dee toh-let-teh) – Where is the bathroom?

8. **Wie viel kostet das?** (vee feel kohs-tet dahs?) – How much does that cost?

9. **Die Rechnung, bitte** (dee reck-noong bit-teh) – The bill, please (when dining)

10. **Ich habe mich verlaufen** (eekh hah-beh meekh fer-lah-fohn) – I'm lost

When dining, the phrase "Ich hätte gern" is particularly helpful when placing orders, while "Wo ist..." works well for asking directions. Make sure to use polite forms such as "Bitte" (please) to show respect. Locals will appreciate your efforts, even if your pronunciation isn't perfect. In tourist-heavy areas, you might find that locals quickly switch to English, but using these basics will enhance your experience

Safety Tips and Staying Secure in Munich

Munich is generally a very safe city, but it's always good to stay aware of your surroundings, especially in busy tourist areas. To ensure a trouble-free trip, keep these tips in mind:

1. **Avoid common scams**: Be cautious around the main tourist hubs like Marienplatz, where pickpockets may operate. Scams such as someone "accidentally" dropping something and asking for help can be used as distractions. Always keep an eye on your belongings, particularly in crowded areas.

2. **Use well-lit areas at night**: Munich is safe to walk at night, but as in any large city, stick to well-lit streets, especially if you're unfamiliar with the area. Schwabing and Glockenbachviertel are lively at night and relatively safe.

3. **Emergency numbers**: For emergencies, dial 112 for medical assistance and fire services, and 110 for police. It's useful to have these stored in your phone.

4. **Solo travelers and families**: Munich is very family-friendly, and solo travelers will feel secure here. However, families should keep an eye on children in

crowded tourist areas and use hotel safes to store valuable documents.

By being mindful of your surroundings and staying in well-traveled areas, you're unlikely to encounter issues. Munich is consistently ranked as one of the safest cities in Europe

Budgeting for Your Trip: Cost Breakdown

The cost of visiting Munich can vary depending on your travel style. Here's an approximate breakdown for 2024-2025:

- **Accommodation**: Budget options like hostels start at €40-€60 per night, while mid-range hotels cost €120-€180 per night. Luxury hotels can range from €350 upwards.

- **Food**: Budget travelers can enjoy meals for about €10-€20 per person at casual restaurants. Mid-range dining will cost €25-€50 per person. For fine dining, expect to spend over €80.

- **Transportation**: A single trip on public transport costs around €3.50, and day passes are €8-€15. If you're staying longer, consider the Deutschland Ticket (€49 per month) for unlimited travel across the country.

- **Attractions**: Entrance fees for major attractions like Nymphenburg Palace or museums can range from €10-€20. If you're planning to visit multiple sites, the Munich City Pass can save you money.

- **Miscellaneous**: Souvenirs and small purchases can add up, so budget an extra €50-€100 for incidentals.

By opting for budget accommodations and public transport, you can comfortably explore Munich for around €100-€150 per day. Mid-range travelers might spend €200-€250 daily.

Currency, Banks, and ATMs

Germany uses the euro (€), and Munich is well-serviced by banks and ATMs. Major credit cards like Visa and Mastercard are widely accepted, though some smaller establishments may only take cash (Bargeld).

- **ATM availability**: You'll find ATMs (Geldautomaten) throughout the city, particularly near major shopping areas and tourist hubs. Deutsche Bank, Commerzbank, and other major banks are good options for reliable ATM services. Many banks charge a €5-€6 fee for international withdrawals, so it's best to check with your bank before traveling.

- **Currency exchange**: Currency exchange services are available at the airport and around the city, but it's often more economical to withdraw euros from an ATM using your credit or debit card. Avoid high-fee currency exchange kiosks.

- **Mobile payments**: Contactless payments using mobile devices like Apple Pay and Google Pay are becoming more popular in Munich, particularly in larger stores, restaurants, and transportation hubs

Health and Travel Insurance

Travel insurance is essential when visiting Munich. Ensure that your policy covers:

- **Medical expenses**: Healthcare in Germany is excellent but can be expensive for non-EU travelers without insurance. Make sure your travel insurance covers emergency medical treatment and repatriation.

- **Accidents and emergencies**: Should you need medical attention, hospitals in Munich are well-equipped, and English-speaking staff are common in larger facilities. Bring your insurance information and a copy of any prescriptions you might need.

- **Pharmacy visits**: Pharmacies (Apotheken) are easy to find, and they can provide medication for minor ailments. Keep your European Health Insurance Card (EHIC) if you're from the EU, or ensure your insurance covers prescriptions.

Should you require urgent medical care, head to the nearest hospital or call 112 for an ambulance. Comprehensive travel insurance will give you peace of mind for any unforeseen issues.

Munich for Families: Kid-Friendly Activities and Tips

Munich offers a wealth of activities for families traveling with children. From interactive museums to sprawling parks, there's something for kids of all ages to enjoy in the city.

One of the most popular destinations is the **Deutsches Museum**, one of the largest science and technology museums in the world. Kids will love the **Kinderreich**, a dedicated section designed for hands-on learning, where they can experiment with water, light, and electricity in an interactive setting. For children interested in space and aviation, the **Deutsches Museum Flugwerft Schleissheim**, located just outside the city, offers exhibits on aircraft and space exploration.

For outdoor fun, head to the **English Garden**, one of Europe's largest urban parks. Families can rent pedal boats on the Kleinhesseloher See or enjoy a picnic in the expansive green spaces. The park also offers playgrounds and plenty of walking and cycling paths. Another excellent outdoor spot is the **Tierpark Hellabrunn**, Munich's Zoo, which offers animal encounters and a petting zoo for younger children. The zoo is organized by continent, making it both educational and fun.

If you're visiting in winter, **Therme Erding**, Europe's largest thermal spa, is a must-visit. With its waterslides, wave pool, and tropical lagoon, it's a hit with both kids and parents. For those looking for indoor activities, **Sea Life Munich** provides an underwater adventure with over 4,500 species, including sharks and sea turtles.

For practical tips, Munich's public transport system is family-friendly, with strollers allowed on trams, buses, and the U-Bahn. Many restaurants in Munich are child-friendly, offering high chairs and kid's menus. Be sure to carry some snacks, as mealtimes in restaurants can be leisurely.

Accessibility in Munich: Tips for Disabled Travelers

Munich is highly accessible for travelers with disabilities, offering a well-organized public transportation system and accessible tourist attractions throughout the city. Whether you're navigating the city by tram, bus, or U-Bahn, you'll find it easy to get around.

Public transportation is equipped for disabled access, with most U-Bahn and S-Bahn stations having elevators and ramps. Additionally, trams and buses are fitted with low floors to accommodate wheelchairs and strollers, and drivers are generally very helpful. **MVV**, Munich's public transport company, provides detailed information on accessibility for each station and vehicle, ensuring a hassle-free journey.

For those visiting key attractions, Munich's famous **Marienplatz** is wheelchair accessible, and many of the city's museums, including the **Alte Pinakothek** and **Deutsches Museum**, are equipped with ramps and elevators. The **Nymphenburg Palace** also offers accessible routes and features, although some parts of the gardens may be more challenging to navigate. If you're visiting in summer, many beer gardens, including those in the **English Garden**, have accessible seating areas.

Hotels in Munich frequently offer accessible rooms, and it's recommended to confirm your specific needs when booking. Some well-known chains like **Hilton** and **Novotel** have fully accessible accommodations with features such as roll-in showers and handrails.

Munich's city center is relatively flat, making it easier for those with mobility impairments to explore on foot or by wheelchair. Maps of the city with accessible routes are available at the **Tourist Information Center** in Marienplatz.

CHAPTER 12: SHOPPING IN MUNICH

Shopping Districts and Streets

Munich offers a vibrant shopping scene, with distinct areas catering to a range of preferences. **Maximilianstrasse** is the pinnacle of luxury, hosting designer stores like Gucci, Louis Vuitton, and Cartier. The street's 19th-century architecture provides a stunning backdrop for this high-end retail experience. For mainstream shopping, head to **Kaufingerstrasse**, Munich's oldest shopping street, known for its department stores and international brands. **Neuhauserstrasse**, another popular pedestrian zone, is a lively hub of shops, ranging from fashion to electronics. For a more bohemian vibe, **Leopoldstrasse** in Schwabing offers quirky boutiques and relaxed cafes, making it a great spot for those looking for something unique. If you enjoy high-end shopping with a cultural twist, **Theatinerstrasse** offers elegant stores amidst historical landmarks. Each district has its distinct flavor, ensuring you'll find whatever you're looking for in Munich's retail landscape.

Traditional Bavarian Souvenirs

Munich is the perfect place to shop for authentic Bavarian souvenirs that reflect the region's cultural heritage. Classic items include **Lederhosen** for men and **Dirndls** for women, traditional outfits perfect for Oktoberfest. For something smaller but equally authentic, **beer steins**—often made from pewter or ceramic—are popular choices. Many can be found at **Hofbräuhaus**, Munich's famous beer hall, or shops around the city. Another iconic souvenir is **Nymphenburg porcelain**, beautifully handcrafted since the 18th century. If you're a foodie, **Lebkuchenherzen** (gingerbread hearts) are popular during the festive season, and you can find them at markets like **Viktualienmarkt**. For those who love spices, **Schuhbecks Gewürze** offers traditional Bavarian spice blends to bring a taste of Munich back home.

Markets and Specialty Stores

For a more local experience, visit **Viktualienmarkt**, Munich's oldest and most famous market, located near Marienplatz. Here, you can browse fresh produce, flowers, and specialty Bavarian foods, from meats and cheeses to artisanal bread. The market also has specialty stalls selling handcrafted items and gourmet treats. Nearby, **Dallmayr Delicatessen** is a must-visit for luxury foods, including chocolates and fine wines. For unique stationery, **Gmund Papier** offers high-quality paper products made in Bavaria. Don't miss **Antiquitäten am Viktualienmarkt** if you're interested in antiques, from vintage jewelry to historical maps.

High-end Boutiques and Designer Shops

If luxury is what you seek, **Maximilianstrasse** is Munich's most prestigious shopping street, home to world-renowned designers like Valentino, Montblanc, and Prada. The street's architectural elegance adds to the charm of high-end shopping. For a more niche luxury experience, visit **Theresa**, where you'll find high-fashion collections from Saint Laurent and Givenchy. Another noteworthy luxury destination is **Lodenfrey**, which combines traditional Bavarian fashion with modern designer pieces across six floors. If you enjoy personalized shopping experiences, **Maffeistrasse** offers boutique shops and exclusive services in a refined setting.

These areas, markets, and boutiques offer a rich variety of shopping experiences, ensuring that you can find both luxurious and traditional treasures in Munich.

CHAPTER 13: LOCAL CUSTOMS AND ETIQUETTE

Bavarian Etiquette: Dos and Don'ts

When visiting Munich, understanding Bavarian etiquette will help you navigate social situations with ease. Bavarians are proud of their culture, which is slightly more formal than other parts of Germany. For greetings, always use "Grüß Gott" (God bless) rather than "Hallo" or "Guten Tag" in Bavarian regions. Handshakes are important and are expected both when meeting someone for the first time and when departing.

When dining, wait until everyone is seated, and a polite "Guten Appetit" should be said before eating. Table manners are crucial; keeping your hands visible on the table (not resting on your lap) is customary. Always use cutlery, and don't rush your meal. Bavaria has strong traditions, and interrupting someone while they are speaking is considered rude, so listen attentively. Bavarians value quietness in public spaces; speaking loudly or engaging in public displays of affection may be frowned upon.

Be punctual, as lateness is seen as disrespectful. When invited to someone's home, it is polite to bring a small gift, such as flowers or chocolates. If you're visiting during one of Munich's many festivals, such as Oktoberfest, pay attention to traditional customs, such as toasting correctly by maintaining eye contact during a "Prost." Bavarians also expect that you separate your waste properly for recycling.

How to Behave in Munich's Beer Halls

Beer halls are an essential part of Munich's culture, but they come with their own set of etiquette. When entering a beer hall, it's common to share tables with strangers, as communal seating is part of the experience. To order beer, simply ask for "ein Maß" (one liter) instead of just asking for a beer. This is especially important during Oktoberfest, where ordering "beer" without specifying the correct size can label you as an outsider.

When clinking glasses, always maintain eye contact and say "Prost." It's a big faux pas to drink before everyone has toasted. If you are enjoying food at the beer hall, don't be shy to ask for local specialties like pretzels or Weisswurst. However, it's considered rude to bring outside food into the hall unless it's a small snack for yourself. Sharing tables with locals is a great way to meet new people, but keep in mind that Bavarians appreciate a balance between friendly conversation and respect for personal space.

Tipping and Service Etiquette

Tipping in Munich is appreciated but not mandatory, and it is generally lower than in other countries like the U.S. At restaurants and cafes, tipping around 5-10% is common for good service. You can round up to the nearest euro, for example, if your bill is €27, you might leave €30. Unlike other places, tips should be given directly to the server when paying, rather than leaving it on the table. For hotels, a tip of €1-2 per bag for the porter and €5 for housekeeping is polite, especially for longer stays. Taxi drivers also appreciate a rounded-up fare or a small tip of about 5%.

Keep in mind that cash is preferred for tipping, even when you pay by card, as it makes it easier for the staff to receive their tip. You can mention the total amount you want to pay (including the tip) directly to the server or taxi driver when handing over the money.

Dress Codes for Various Occasions

In Munich, dress codes vary depending on the occasion. For day-to-day activities, casual attire is widely accepted, especially if you're sightseeing or exploring the city. However, Bavarians dress more formally for dinners, business meetings, or religious events. For such occasions, men should wear trousers with a collared shirt, and women might choose a blouse with a skirt or slacks.

If you're visiting a church, such as the famous Frauenkirche, avoid wearing shorts or sleeveless tops, as it's considered disrespectful. Festivals like Oktoberfest, on the other hand, are the perfect opportunity to don traditional clothing. Men typically wear **Lederhosen**, while women wear **Dirndls**. These outfits are not just for show; they are a proud part of the Bavarian heritage and are widely worn during the event. The position of a Dirndl's bow is symbolic—tying it on the right means you're taken while tying it on the left signals you're single.

Being mindful of these dress expectations will ensure that you blend in and show respect for Bavarian traditions while enjoying your time in Munich.

CHAPTER 14: INSIDER TIPS FOR FIRST-TIME VISITORS TO MUNICH

Avoiding Tourist Traps

When visiting Munich for the first time, it's tempting to hit all the well-known spots like Marienplatz and Hofbräuhaus. However, these areas can be crowded, and some consider them to be tourist traps, especially during peak season. For a more authentic experience, opt for alternatives like **Hofbräukeller** on Wiener Platz or **Augustiner-Keller**, which offer a more local vibe and equally good Bavarian food. Additionally, while the glockenspiel at Marienplatz is a famous sight, standing around for the entire performance might feel underwhelming. Consider watching it online or just passing by to enjoy the architecture and explore the side streets of the **Altstadt (Old Town)**. For shopping, avoid the souvenir-heavy areas around Marienplatz and instead, explore the artisan shops around **Gärtnerplatz** for unique finds. Always double-check restaurant prices in tourist-heavy areas, as they can be inflated compared to those in quieter neighborhoods.

How to Skip the Lines at Major Attractions

Munich is home to some must-see attractions like the **Munich Residenz, Nymphenburg Palace**, and the **BMW Museum**. To save time and avoid long queues, book tickets online in advance. For the **Munich Residenz**, the combination ticket (covering the museum, treasury, and Cuvilliés Theatre) offers the best value and can be purchased at the **Cuvilliés Theatre** entrance, where the lines are usually shorter. The same goes for **Nymphenburg Palace**—book a skip-the-line tour to avoid the crowds at the ticket office. Some attractions, like the **BMW Museum**, offer timed entry tickets, so plan your visit early in the morning or late in the afternoon to beat the crowds.

Munich on a Budget: How to Save Money

Munich can be an expensive city, but there are plenty of ways to experience it on a budget. Public transportation is efficient and affordable, especially if you buy a **Tageskarte (day ticket)**, which offers unlimited travel on the U-Bahn, S-Bahn, trams, and buses. If you're planning a longer stay, consider the **Deutschland-Ticket**, which provides unlimited travel across all public transport in Germany for €49 per month. For budget dining, skip the touristy beer halls and head to the local markets like **Viktualienmarkt**, where you can sample fresh Bavarian produce and grab a meal at one of the food stalls. Many museums, such as the **Pinakothek Museums**, offer discounted entry on Sundays, with tickets as low as €1. Finally, explore Munich's free attractions, such as the **English Garden**, **Olympiapark**, and the many historical churches like **Frauenkirche** and **St. Peter's Church**.

CHAPTER 16: IMPORTANT INFORMATION FOR TOURISTS

Emergency Contacts and Hospitals

In Munich, emergency services are accessible through the European emergency numbers. If you face a critical situation, dial **112** for ambulance services, fire department, or emergency medical assistance. For police assistance in any emergency, dial **110**. Both numbers are available free of charge, 24/7.

Munich is equipped with excellent hospitals that provide emergency services. Key hospitals include:

- **Schwabing Hospital** (Kölner Platz 1, 80804 Munich) specializes in adult and pediatric emergency care and offers 24-hour medical services. Contact: +49 89 3068 2359.

- **Harlaching Hospital** (Sanatoriumsplatz 2, 81545 Munich) is another reliable choice for both surgical and internal medical emergencies. Contact: +49 89 6210 2333.

- **Bogenhausen Hospital** (Englschalkinger Str. 77, 81925 Munich) provides surgery and emergency services. Contact: +49 89 9270 2150.

For English-speaking tourists, most hospitals have multilingual staff or translators available. Additionally, 24-hour pharmacies and pediatric care are available across the city, such as **Dr. von Hauner's Children's Hospital** (Lindwurmstr. 4, 80337 Munich), which specializes in child care. For poison emergencies, contact the **Munich Poison Control Centre** at +49 89 19240.

Tourist Information Centers

Munich's tourist information centers are vital for visitors. The main center is located in **Marienplatz**, right in the heart of the city. Open daily from 9 a.m. to 7 p.m., they offer services like maps, guided tours, and booking assistance. They also provide multilingual support, with information available in English, German, Spanish, and French. Whether you need help navigating public transport or booking a day trip to Neuschwanstein Castle, these centers are equipped to assist. There's also a tourist center at the **Munich Central Station (Hauptbahnhof)**, open from 9 a.m. to 6 p.m. daily.

Local Police

Tourists in Munich can rely on the professionalism and efficiency of the local police. In an emergency, dial **110**, which will connect you to the nearest police station. For non-emergencies, such as reporting a lost item or minor incidents, you can call the general non-emergency number **089 6216 0**. Munich's police stations are distributed across the city, with the main station located at **Ettstr. 2-4, 80333 Munich**. Additionally, there is a dedicated **Tourist Police Unit** near Marienplatz that provides assistance specifically tailored to travelers.

Pharmacies

Pharmacies, known as **Apotheke**, are easy to find in Munich. Most are open Monday through Saturday from 8 a.m. to 6:30 p.m., with some remaining open until later. For after-hours service, you can use the 24-hour pharmacy hotline at **+49 89 594 475**, or check online for a nearby pharmacy on duty. These pharmacies provide both prescription and over-the-counter medications, including remedies for common ailments like colds, headaches, or digestive issues. Look for the green "A" sign, which designates licensed pharmacies across the city. For prescription refills, bring your doctor's prescription to any pharmacy for fulfillment.

CONCLUSION

As we come to the end of this *Munich Travel Guide 2025*, I want to take a moment to thank you for choosing this book as your companion for your journey through one of Europe's most vibrant and historic cities. Whether you're a first-time visitor or returning to explore more of Munich's charm, this guide has been crafted with the hope of enhancing your experience, helping you navigate the city with ease, and uncovering the magic in both its famous landmarks and hidden corners.

Throughout this book, we've covered the essentials from iconic attractions like Marienplatz, the English Garden, and Nymphenburg Palace, to insider tips on where to find the best food, cultural experiences, and hidden gems. You've discovered ways to get around the city efficiently, whether by public transport, biking, or simply walking through the picturesque streets. We've also explored unique places to stay, from luxury hotels to budget-friendly accommodations, catering to every type of traveler.

As you take on this adventure, may your time in Munich be filled with memorable moments, whether you're enjoying a local pretzel at Viktualienmarkt, marveling at the grandeur of the Bavarian architecture, or relaxing in one of the city's peaceful gardens. I pray that your journey will be safe, fulfilling, and filled with joy as you create lasting memories.

Travel is one of the greatest ways to connect with the world and grow in appreciation for its beauty and diversity. I hope this guide has been a valuable resource, helping you make the most of your stay in Munich. May your travels be blessed with discoveries, meaningful encounters, and an abundance of wonderful experiences. Safe travels and may you return home inspired, enriched, and eager for your next adventure!

BONUS

Munich Photo Challenge

If you're planning a trip to Munich in 2024-2025 and want to capture the essence of this vibrant city, the *Munich Photo Challenge* is the perfect way to do so. From iconic landmarks to hidden gems, this challenge will take you through must-see spots and less-traveled paths for an unforgettable visual journey. Here's a curated list of 25 must-take photos along with a special hashtag (#MunichPhotoChallenge2025) to share your experiences with fellow travelers.

1. **Marienplatz and the New Town Hall (Neues Rathaus)**: The heart of Munich, featuring the famous Glockenspiel. Arrive early to avoid crowds and capture the intricate details of the Gothic architecture.

2. **St. Peter's Church (Alter Peter)**: Climb the tower for panoramic views of Munich's red-roofed cityscape and the distant Alps.

3. **Viktualienmarkt**: This bustling market is perfect for foodie shots. Don't forget to snap a picture with a giant Bavarian pretzel!

4. **Nymphenburg Palace Gardens**: Capture the grandeur of this historic palace, especially the stunning Temple of Apollo nestled in its gardens.

5. **English Garden (Englischer Garten)**: Snap photos of locals relaxing by the Chinese Tower beer garden, or catch surfers riding the waves at the Eisbach river.

6. **Odeonsplatz and Theatinerkirche**: This stunning Baroque church and square make for a perfect blend of architectural beauty and lively city life.

7. **Hofgarten**: The idyllic Renaissance-style Garden is perfect for peaceful, nature-filled shots, especially around the Dianatempel gazebo.

8. **BMW Museum**: Car enthusiasts should capture the sleek, modern lines of this building and the impressive displays of BMW history.

9. **St. Paul's Church**: Best visited during Oktoberfest, this neo-Gothic church offers spectacular views from its tower.

10. **Müller'sches Volksbad**: Take a unique shot of this Art Nouveau public bathhouse, especially its stunning interior.

11. **Königsplatz**: Known for its Greek-inspired architecture, this neoclassical square offers a striking backdrop for historical photos.

12. **Alte Pinakothek**: For art lovers, capture the grand staircase or the impressive galleries housing old masters' works.

13. **Olympiapark**: Climb the Olympic Hill for sweeping views of the park and the famous Olympic Tower.

14. **Maximilianeum**: The seat of the Bavarian Parliament offers magnificent views over the Isar River and makes for an impressive photo at sunset.

15. **Residenz Munich**: Snap the ornate interiors of this former royal palace, especially the Antiquarium hall, one of the most opulent rooms in Munich.

16. **Bavarian National Museum**: If you're a fan of Bavarian history, this museum offers great indoor shots of intricate art and cultural relics.

17. **Pinakothek der Moderne**: A must for modern art lovers, the clean lines of this museum provide fantastic architectural shots.

18. **Propylaea at Königsplatz**: This Greek-inspired gateway is one of Munich's most photogenic spots, particularly at sunset.

19. **Isartor Gate**: One of Munich's medieval city gates, perfect for history buffs looking to capture the remnants of the city's ancient fortifications.

20. **Eisbachwelle**: For something different, capture surfers riding the artificial wave in the middle of the English Garden.

21. **Bavaria Statue at Theresienwiese**: Snap a shot with this massive statue, especially during Oktoberfest when the area is filled with festive energy.

22. **Asam Church (Asamkirche)**: A lesser-known Baroque gem, this small but ornate church is a treasure for architectural photography.

23. **Gärtnerplatz**: Capture the vibrant life of this square, full of cafés, restaurants, and locals enjoying Munich's laid-back vibe.

24. **Hackerbrücke at Sunset**: This bridge offers a perfect vantage point for sunset shots of Munich's skyline.

25. **Schwabing's Art Nouveau Houses**: Wander through Schwabing to find beautiful Art Nouveau façades, especially along Ainmillerstrasse and Isabellastraße.

By completing the *Munich Photo Challenge*, not only will you capture the city's famous sights, but you'll also uncover hidden treasures that will make your trip—and your photos—unique. Share your moments with #MunichPhotoChallenge2025 to connect with other travelers and showcase your journey.